turning the
tables
on las vegas

turning the tables on las vegas

Ian Andersen

VINTAGE BOOKS
A DIVISION OF RANDOM HOUSE
NEW YORK

FIRST VINTAGE BOOKS EDITION, February 1978

Library of Congress Cataloging in Publication Data

Andersen, Ian.
  Turning the tables on Las Vegas.

  1. Cardsharping. 2. Gambling—Nevada—Las Vegas.
  I. Title.
[GV1247.A53 1978]   795   77–14286
ISBN 0–394–72509–3

Manufactured in the United States of America

D9876

I staked (my last) gulden on manque. . . . There really is something special in the feeling when, alone, in a strange country, far away from home and friends and not knowing what you will eat that day, you stake your last gulden, your very, very last! I won, and twenty minutes later . . . left with 170 gulden in my pocket. That is a fact! You see what one's last gulden may sometimes mean! And what if I had lost courage then, if I had not dared to decide!

Tomorrow, tomorrow it will all come to an end!

From THE GAMBLER by
Fyodor Dostoyevsky

TABLE OF CONTENTS

$

Foreword

The purpose of this book is to enable the reader to learn a winning strategy in gambling games, and also to provide factual anecdotes that the reader will, I hope, find beneficial, interesting, and amusing. For the reader to turn the tables on Las Vegas he must have not only a viable playing strategy for blackjack and poker, but a thorough understanding of the psychological and motivational aspects of the players, the dealers, the pit bosses, and the casino executives. From this book you will gain a thorough understanding of the flavor of Las Vegas, how the system works, and how to beat it. You will learn a psychological approach and develop a demeanor that will optimize your playing conditions and maximize your winnings.

I have tried to capture and relate the essence of Las Vegas—the glamor, the shows, the women, the gambling, the gourmet restaurants—as I have lived them.

This books also attempts to alert you to potential traps, some within the Las Vegas system and some within you as a human being, and to teach you how to avoid these pitfalls.

It emphasizes self-discipline and teaches the reader how to cope with the inevitable stresses and still maintain composure.

It teaches camouflage–not by being devious, but by understanding the persons with whom you are interacting and filling their needs.

In short, this book outlines the makings of a symbiotic relationship between you as a winning player and a hierarchy of casino personnel, each with his own needs. In this way everyone wins except the large corporations that currently own the major Las Vegas casinos.

The objective of TURNING THE TABLES ON LAS VEGAS is to present a *total* strategy for playing twenty-one (blackjack) and other games of chance. Chapters two and three respectively deal with the mechanics and playing tactics for twenty-one, both of which are extremely important concepts, but away from the main thrust of this book. Readers already familiar with these concepts may well choose to skim these two chapters.

turning the
tables
on las vegas

1

The Flavor of
Las Vegas

Las Vegas is one of the most unusual cities in the world. Located in the heart of the Mojave Desert, its complex of enormous, grandiose hotels and expensive neon signs seem like a strange anachronism. The town was founded by gangland families from Detroit (the Purple Gang), Cleveland, and New York, with the express purpose of creating a gambling oasis in the desert. And the city has grown at a furious rate: ten years ago the population was 80,000; today its population is over 300,000 and still expanding.

Although "hit" men and muggers can still be found, the mob element is slowly being replaced by legitimate corporate enterprises, led by Howard Hughes's Summa Corporation, seeking diversification into gambling. Lum's, MGM, Recrion, Continental Connectors, and Hilton have all owned Las Vegas hotels and casinos. New casinos are constructed on a regular basis and old ones are constantly remodeled, with new wings being added to accommodate greater numbers of guests. Las Vegas has become a favorite site for conventions, as

1

many of the large hotels sport lavish convention facilities. The major hotels have between 1,500 and 2,000 rooms and they are 100 percent occupied on a busy weekend. Opulence abounds, as each facility competes for players. Every entrance leads through the casino. In order to get to the restaurants, shows, arcades of shops, beauty salons, and health spas you must enter and leave through the casino. It is open twenty-four hours a day and there are no clocks. If you must catch a plane, you had better have your own watch. Casinos are hoping you will lose track of time, miss your plane, and lose some more money. Everything is designed to attract and keep the player gambling.

A multitude of headliners perform in Las Vegas. Stars like Frank Sinatra, Sammy Davis Jr., Tom Jones, Elvis Presley, and Bill Cosby are common. Entertainers are paid as much as $150,000 a week, as the casinos aggressively bid for the available talent. A recent additional attraction has been major sports events: Caesar's Palace has hosted challenge tennis matches featuring Jimmy Connors (most recently for a $250,000 winner-take-all match); Muhammed Ali defended his title in Las Vegas; and there are frequent major golf tournaments.

Numerous gourmet restaurants are scattered through the hotels, offering myriad delicacies. Live Maine lobster, fresh clams, and oysters are flown in daily to the Dome of the Sea at the Dunes Hotel. The Bacchanal Room at Caesar's Palace features gluttony at its finest —a ten-course dinner complete with four different wines decanted by sparsely clad wine "goddesses." The wine girl doubles as masseuse and gently rubs away your headache from overindulgence, your head cradled securely in her pneumatic bosom. French, Italian, Japanese, delicatessen—you name it; it can be found in Las Vegas.

For those interested in something a bit more spicy, prostitutes are readily available. Although illegal in Clark County, which incorporates Las Vegas, prostitution flourishes. It is estimated that four thousand hookers live in the Las Vegas area. Women (or men, for that matter) can easily be obtained by asking any hotel bell captain or bellman. Three or four can usually be found sitting at the bar in most major casinos. The going rate is $100 per hour, although some of the bar girls can be persuaded to share their charms for $50 if business is slow. For those who still blanch at the tariff, old-fashioned streetwalkers are plentiful and often proposition men on the Las Vegas Strip.* Although somewhat less appealing than the *haute couture* beauties who frequent the hotels, a decent *belle de rue* can be leased for $25 for a brief interlude.

Las Vegas attracts a curious clientele. It seems as though every used-car salesman in the world has taken up permanent residence in the Strip hotels. Women shed their conventional attire in favor of knee-high purple boots and hot pants. Everything goes—it's fast, it's fun, and it's loose, so visitors "let it all hang out." Those who are gambling are plied with free drinks that douse any remaining inhibitions. Forget everything and "let 'er rip," and so they do.

The restaurants, shows, bars, and lavish casinos create an exciting atmosphere. People's eyes sparkle with eager anticipation and exhilaration. Money quickly loses importance. Everything is overpriced, and in a remarkably short period of time a ten-dollar bill seems

* The area that includes all of the Las Vegas luxury hotels is known as the Strip. This excludes the downtown casinos.

like a dime. People are hustling in every direction, and the tables are usually crowded with expectant players. In this environment it is easy to feel "lucky," and the rewards appear to far outweigh the risks. After all, they can only win your bank roll, say $200, while you could win a million. "It's worth a shot," you say as you squeeze to a table. It's this behavior, this false confidence, that feeds Las Vegas. The town flourishes on the money you lose gambling, and each establishment subtly creates the appropriate atmosphere, with attention to every nuance. They even make you feel good about your loss. The pit boss is more than eager to commiserate with you—"Boy, you really had some bad luck; I don't think you won two hands in a row all night." The cocktail waitress also sympathizes with your plight, "How about another drink? I'll order my special; it will make you feel better." Surprisingly, this support does salve the sting of losing. There are plenty of other losers around and, after all, you are *supposed* to lose in Las Vegas. Anyway, it was a lot of fun. Maybe next time you'll make that big score.

And so the town continues to grow, feeding your hedonistic needs in exchange for your dollars.

We're about to change all that.

2

An Introduction
to Blackjack

Winning gambling is an art. Before moving into the interesting subtleties of twenty-one (blackjack) and other games, you have to know the rules. Unfortunately, this is dry stuff and those of you who are familiar with blackjack could well skip to the next chapter.

In blackjack each player plays against the dealer. Tables accommodate one to seven players. Depending upon the casino, one, two, or four decks of cards are used. The deck(s) are shuffled and the top card is removed and placed face up on the bottom of the deck. This card is called the "burn" card. Players are usually prevented from seeing the "burn" card.

Next, the player makes his bet. The rules of each casino vary as to the minimum and maximum wagers. The minimum range is currently 50¢ to $2. The maximum range is $200 to $2,000. The Strip hotels generally have the highest minimums and maximums. On occasion the house will raise the limit for "high rollers." A "high roller" is an exceedingly wealthy individual with a large credit limit. These people are capable of

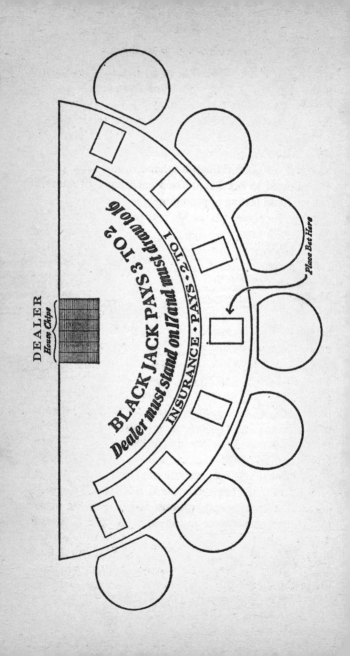

winning or losing $500,000 to $1,000,000 in a single night. Some major casinos are now raising their maximum bets proportionate to a player's bank roll.* I have seen one man bet $3,000 at all seven stations in twenty-one. His risk on each deal was $21,000 minimum. At times, given some of the available playing options, he had over $30,000 riding on a hand. (This same person was allowed to bet $12,000 on each hand of baccarat —each hand lasting approximately twelve seconds!)

After the player places his bet, he is dealt two cards face down. The dealer gets one card face down and turns his second card face up. Table 1 shows the playing value of each card.

The object is for the player to get closer to twenty-one than the dealer without exceeding it ("breaking"). The two cards are added together. The player always acts first. He can "stand" by placing the two cards beneath his bet, or he can "hit" by scratching the table with his two cards. A third card will be dealt face up when the player hits. The player can continue to hit until he no longer desires additional cards or exceeds the 21 limit. If the player exceeds 21, he must turn all his cards face up. His bet is immediately forfeited. After all players have acted on their hands the dealer acts. Unlike the player, the dealer must act without choice. If his cards total 16 or less, he must hit.

When the dealer's total equals 17 or more, he must stand. The only exception to this rule is when the dealer has an ace and one or more cards totaling 6—a soft

* At the Horseshoe Casino in downtown Las Vegas there is "no limit" in craps. Your first bet is the limit. If it is $30,000 that is your limit. This interesting wrinkle allows the player to set his own limit.

17.* Since aces may be valued as 1 or 11, his total is either 17 or 7. At the Strip casinos in Las Vegas, the dealer must stand on soft 17. In downtown Las Vegas, Lake Tahoe, and Reno, the dealer must hit soft 17. It is advantageous to the player for the dealer to stand on soft 17.

TABLE 1

Card	Value
Ace	1 or 11
King Queen Jack 10	All valued at 10
9 8 7 6 5 4 3 2	All at face value (9 valued at 9, 6 valued at 6, etc.)

If the player is dealt an ace and a 10-value card, he has a natural 21. Unless the dealer also has a natural 21, the player is immediately paid one and a half times his bet. When the house is dealt an untied natural 21, all player bets are immediately forfeit.

When the dealer's up card is an ace, the player can "insure" his hand against the dealer having a natural 21. To do this he places an amount equal to one-half

---

* A soft hand is one that includes an ace, in which the ace may be valued at 1 or 11, without the total exceeding 21, when the ace is valued at 11.

his original bet in front of the circle containing his wager. Insurance pays 2 to 1. If the dealer's down card is a 10-value card, the player loses his original bet but wins his insurance bet. This results in a break-even situation. If the dealer does not have a 10 in the hole, the insurance bet is lost and the hand is played out like any other hand for the original wager.

The player has several options not available to the dealer. He may double down and he may split pairs. To double down, both cards are turned face up and the amount of the bet is doubled. One card is then dealt face down. The rules prevent the player from drawing additional cards. The dealer then acts on his hand. In Las Vegas, doubling down is permitted on *any* two cards. Combinations totaling 10 and 11 are obvious doubling situations, but it is often correct to double with 9 or 8 or with a combination of an ace and another card. (Doubling down using an ace and any other card is called soft doubling.) The dealer's up card and the composition of the remaining cards are important factors in determining whether or not to double down.

When the player is dealt a pair, he may split it. To accomplish this he separates the two matched cards face up on the table and places an additional bet equal to his original amount behind the second card. He now is effectively playing two hands. Each hand is then played by the standard rules. (In some casinos doubling down after splitting a pair is allowed. For example, if the player is dealt 8–8 and splits, and is given a 3 on the first 8, he may choose to double down on this hand in the manner previously described. This rule is an advantage to the player and should not be overlooked.)

Some casinos offer another player option called surrender. After the deal—but *before* the player acts on his hand—he may forfeit one-half of his bet without playing out the hand. Although this is often a sucker's play, it can be most advantageous to the sophisticated player. In some situations half a bet can be saved when normally the player would surely lose his entire bet. For example, you are dealt 16 and the dealer has a 10 up. You happen to know the remaining cards in the deck are all 10's, so there is now no way you can win. The dealer surely has 20. If you draw, you will get a 10, giving you 26—a bust. By surrendering, you lose only one-half your bet, a *fifty percent saving!*

The casino advantage is derived from the fact that the player must always act first. But the player has flexibility on his side. He may buy insurance, split pairs, double down, or surrender. He has the option of either hitting or standing on any total. He is paid three for two when he gets blackjack—the dealer only takes his bet on a house blackjack. Most important, the player can vary his bet at the start of each new hand.

This flexibility actually gives the knowledgeable player an *overall* advantage. In blackjack, the odds change with each deal. As cards are eliminated from play the advantage will fluctuate. When 9's, 10's, and aces are used up, the advantage will swing toward the house. As 2, 3, 4, 5, 6, 7 are removed, the odds move in favor of the player. By recognizing when he has the advantage and betting and playing accordingly, the player can win consistently at twenty-one.

All successful strategies depend upon betting the amount appropriate to the composition of the cards remaining in the deck.

The next chapter reviews current systems that give the player a significant advantage. This edge can actually exceed that enjoyed by the house over a respectable non-system player. Learning a winning system takes a little work, but I know of no greater return for time invested.

3

A Review of Blackjack Systems

Blackjack is the only casino game in which the odds are constantly changing. Each hand is an independent event with the odds sometimes favoring the casino and sometimes the player. The composition of the remaining cards determines the odds on the next hand. The cards that have been used are reshuffled only when a few cards remain unplayed. All winning twenty-one systems depend upon knowing when the player has the advantage and increasing the size of the bet in these situations. By making small bets when the deck favors the house and larger bets when the deck favors the player, the card counter will win overall. He may lose more bets than he wins, but he will tend to win the big bets and lose the smaller ones.

It is not my intention to present an exhaustive analysis of the various published twenty-one count strategies. They all work! I have heard lengthy debates by counters, each espousing different systems. Every counter thinks his method is the best. Any good system that is thoroughly mastered and works for you is the best one to use. Your winning rate may be $400 per hour instead of $500 per hour, but worse things can happen.

It is imperative that you do master one of the count strategies, but it is more important to learn how to manipulate casino conditions to maximize your playing advantage and preserve your longevity as a player. This is the main objective of this book. A brief review of the available twenty-one strategies is warranted to better enable you to choose the one best suited to your needs, but once you make a selection, stick with it and perfect it. Jumping from one strategy to another is an unnecessary distraction.

The first published twenty-one count strategy was devised in the early 1960s by Professor Edward Thorp *et al*. They discovered that the greater the number of 10-value cards remaining in the deck, the better the player's chances of winning. The logic behind this concept is clear. The house derives its advantage from the fact that the player must always act first. If the player's total exceeds 21, his bet is lost. Several options compensate the player for this disadvantage—doubling down, splitting pairs, surrender (when available), and the option of whether to draw or stand. In addition, the bettor is paid a hundred and fifty percent of his wager when he has blackjack. When the percentage of 10's increases, these options become more valuable, since the probability of breaking increases proportionately to the number of remaining 10's. Since the dealer *must* draw on 16 or less, regardless of the number of remaining 10's, the player can capitalize on the increased chance of the dealer breaking. This advantage can be broken down as follows:

1) The player can stand on totals of 12–16; the dealer must draw.

2) The player can double down, doubling the size of his bet when advantageous; the dealer can only draw. The benefit of a large number of 10's remaining for doubling on starting hands of 10 or 11 is obvious, but they are also beneficial for totals of 9 or 8, and for soft doubling combinations,* when the dealer shows a small card and is likely to break.

3) The player can split pairs, which serves to increase the size of his bet and change bad hands into good ones (for example, splitting 8–8 and having two hands with a value of 8 instead of one hand equaling 16). The dealer does not enjoy this advantage. (In this example he must draw to the 16 and will probably break.) Splitting pairs is especially beneficial as the dealer's chances of breaking increase. In casinos where doubling down after splitting is permitted, the advantage of a 10-rich deck is further increased.

4) The player gets paid a hundred and fifty percent for a natural 21 (blackjack), but the house only wins the amount bet. Since blackjacks require 10-value cards, a surplus of 10's increases the probability of blackjacks–another player advantage.

5) When the dealer shows an ace, you can buy insurance. Since you are insuring against a dealer blackjack, insurance is indeed very profitable in 10-rich decks.

So, for all these reasons, the player's advantage increases when a surplus of 10's remains.

Dr. Thorp devised his "10 Count" strategy around this knowledge. He set up a ratio of "non-10's" (all other cards except 10's) to 10's. When the deck con-

---

* When the dealer is likely to break, it pays to double with an ace and a small card (e.g., ace/6 when the dealer shows a small card and the deck is full of 10's).

tains a greater proportion of 10-value cards, he increases the size of his bet. He also alters the play of each hand depending upon this ratio.*

Thorp's 10-count system works. I used it in 1968 with good success. It suffers, however, from two disadvantages. First, it misses many profitable betting situations; second, it is difficult for the player to camouflage the fact that he is using a count strategy, because wide variations in bet size are required—a fatal flaw. (See next chapter.)

Count strategies took a quantum leap forward as a result of the work of Dr. Julian Braun of the IBM Corporation. Braun analyzed the value of each card and found that a surplus of 9's, 10's and aces favored the player. A surplus of small-value cards favors the house. The most important card for the player is the ace because of its blackjack potential; the most important card for the house is the 5 because it changes all bad hands into good ones (12–16 becomes 17–21 respectively).

Dr. Braun developed several count strategies by assigning a plus or minus value to each card. His first simple point-count system is published in Thorp's version of *Beat the Dealer*. Dr. Braun then collaborated with Lawrence Revere, and some of his more sophisticated strategies are published in Revere's book *Playing Blackjack as a Business*.

In essence, Braun's system works as follows. At the beginning of each deck the count is zero. As each card is exposed and removed from play, its assigned value is added or subtracted and a running total is kept. Most active blackjack players use some version of this plus-

* For a complete description of Professor Thorp's system, see *Beat the Dealer*, Random House.

minus system. The variation that I currently use in casino play places the following values on each card:

TABLE 2

2,3,4,6,7,	—	plus 1
5	—	plus 2
8	—	zero
9,10,J,Q,K,	—	minus 1
Ace	—	minus 2

With typical Las Vegas rules, any plus count tips the odds in favor of the player; a zero count is a neutral situation; and any minus count favors the house. The higher the plus count, the greater the player's advantage; the higher the minus count, the greater the house advantage.

Betting Strategy vs. Playing Strategy

Most published count strategies fail to distinguish between a betting strategy and a playing strategy. These are really separate issues. Any plus deck is a fruitful betting situation. But after the cards are dealt, the betting count is no longer applicable. The most important reason for this is the value of the ace. In Table 1 the ace is given a value of minus 2. It is the single most important card for the player, with an equivalent weight of two 10-value cards. The ace is weighted in this manner primarily because of its blackjack potential (natural 21). Since the player is paid one hundred and fifty percent of his bet for a natural, aces are of supreme importance. They are also important for soft doubling, which further adds to their weighted value. But beyond these two circumstances, the playing value of the ace plummets. To hands like 11, 12, 13, 14, and 15 the ace is actually a liability; it adds only slight value to 16. It is clear, then, that for playing purposes the value of the ace diminishes.

I keep a separate count of aces. The normal distribution of aces would be one per quarter of a deck. Obviously, this statistical norm does not always hold true. Sometimes the remaining cards are proportionately rich or poor in aces. For example, if one-fourth of the deck has been played and all four aces remain, then the deck is rich (extra) by one ace; if one-fourth of the deck has been played and only two aces remain, then the deck is poor by one ace. How, then, does this affect the count for *playing* purposes? I *subtract* 2 from the count for each "extra" ace and I *add* 2 to the count for each "missing" ace. This is for playing purposes only! When the next hand is dealt, I revert back to my basic betting count. I modify it temporarily during each hand for playing purposes by referring to my ring.* This modification is only a reflection of the impact of aces on the play of each hand.

An *ideal* playing strategy requires knowledge of all the remaining cards in the deck. Given a starting hand of 12, there is a big difference between drawing a 9 (21) and drawing a 10 (22), even though both cards have a value of minus 1. The playing system I currently use varies, depending on the composition of the remaining cards. In this example, I would draw to 12 if the dealer showed a deuce with a playing count of plus

* For this purpose I use my finger ring. I rotate it one quarter turn each time an ace is played.

4 and half a deck remaining, if I knew that all four 9's were left in the deck. If only one, two, or three 9's remain, I would stand.

Although it is an added advantage to have a precise playing strategy for each situation, it is far from imperative. Such a perfect strategy could only be implemented with the use of a computer. An approximation, using a plus-minus count and correcting for aces, is more than sufficient. I recommend the Revere Advanced Plus-Minus Strategy * or the Hi-Opt System.** These systems both incorporate a betting and playing strategy with substantial profit expectation. Both of these sophisticated systems were computed by Julian Braun, and are more accurate than the published 10-count and simple point-count systems. I prefer to use my count (Table 2) and the playing strategy set forth in Tables 3–7.

Regardless of which count system you choose, master it thoroughly and stick with it. Remember, they *all* work. Betting from one to four units, your win rate will vary from 1.5 percent to 2.3 percent of total dollars bet. When you are the only player at the table, you can play about one hundred hands per hour. With an average bet of $200 a hand, your win rate will vary from $300 per hour to $460 per hour. With a perfect playing strategy you may increase this figure to $525–$550 per hour. But these differences are relatively unimportant. It wouldn't matter if your rate of return was $10,000 per hour if the casinos refused to let you play. So learn any of the strategies mentioned, then focus on diverting at-

* Available from Lawrence Revere, 1517 Rexford Place, Las Vegas, Nevada, 89104 ($25).

** Available from International Gaming Incorporated, 25 Johnson Avenue, Thornhill, Ontario, Canada ($200).

tention from what you are doing. More important than straining after a "perfect" strategy is your longevity as a player.

You may know a system perfectly, but being able to utilize it is an altogether different story.

TABLE 3

HARD STANDING NUMBERS

I stand if the playing count equals or is more positive than the number in box

I have: ↓	Dealer's Up Card									
	2	3	4	5	6	7	8	9	10	A
12	+2	+1	−1	−3	−2	H	H	H	H	H
13	−1	−2	−3	−5	−4	H	H	H	H	H
14	−3	−4	−5	−7	−6	H	H	H	H	H
15	−6	−7	−8	S	S	H	H	+5	+2	H
16	−8	S	S	S	S	H	H	+4	0	+6
17 & Up	Always stand									

S = always stand
H = always hit

TABLE 4

DOUBLING DOWN

I double if the count equals or is more positive than the number in box

I have: ↓	Dealer's Up Card									
	2	3	4	5	6	7	8	9	10	A
11	D	D	D	D	D	−7	−5	−4	−3	0
10	D	D	D	D	D	−6	−4	−1	+4	+3
9	+1	0	−2	−4	−4	+3	H	H	H	H
8	H	H	+5	+3	+3	H	H	H	H	H
A,9	S	S	+7	+5	+5	S	S	S	S	S
A,8	+7	+4	+2	+1	+1	S	S	S	S	S
A,7	+1	−1	−5	−6	−7	S	S	H	H	−1
A,6	+1	−2	−5	D	D	H	H	H	H	H
A,5	H	+3	−1	−6	D	H	H	H	H	H
A,4	H	+3	−1	−5	−8	H	H	H	H	H
A,3	H	+5	0	−3	−5	H	H	H	H	H
A,2	H	+5	+1	−2	−3	H	H	H	H	H

D = always double down   S = always stand
H = always hit

TABLE 5

SPLITTING PAIRS

I split pairs when the count equals or is more positive than the number in the box

I have: ↓	Dealer's Up Card									
	2	3	4	5	6	7	8	9	10	A
AA	Sp	Sp	Sp	Sp	Sp	Sp	−8	−7	−7	−4
22	+7	+2	−2	−6	Sp	Sp	H	H	H	H
33	+8	+5	0	−2	Sp	Sp	H	H	H	H
66	+2	0	−1	−4	−6	H	H	H	H	H
77	Sp	Sp	Sp	Sp	Sp	Sp	H	H	0H*	H
88	Sp	Sp	Sp	Sp	Sp	Sp	Sp	Sp	6**	Sp
99	−1	−2	−3	−5	−4	+6	Sp	Sp	S	+5

* STAND if the count is zero or greater; otherwise hit.
** STAND if the count is plus 6 or greater; otherwise split.

Sp = always split   H = always hit
S = always stand

NOTE: Never split 5,5. Although it is technically correct to split 10's in certain circumstances, this play draws so much attention that it should hardly ever be used.

TABLE 6

SPLITTING PAIRS
WHEN PLAYER CAN DOUBLE AFTER SPLITTING

I split when the count equals or is more positive than the numbers in the box

I have: ↓	Dealer's Up Card									
	2	3	4	5	6	7	8	9	10	A
AA	SAME AS TABLE 5									
22	−4	−5	Sp	Sp	Sp	Sp	H	H	H	H
33	−2	−4	Sp	Sp	Sp	Sp	H	H	H	H
44	H	H	3	1	0	H	H	H	H	H
66	−1	−3	−4	Sp	Sp	H	H	H	H	H
77	Sp	Sp	Sp	Sp	Sp	Sp	−1	SAME AS TABLE 5		
88	SAME AS TABLE 5									
99	−2	−3	−4	−6	−5	+4	Sp	Sp	S	+4

H = always hit   Sp = always split
S = always stand

TABLE 7

I SURRENDER (WHEN ALLOWED)

I surrender if the count equals or is more positive than the number in the box

I have: ↓	Dealer's Up Card			
	8	**9**	**10**	**A**
16	+4	+1	−1	0
15	+6	+2	0	+1
14	H	+5	+2	+6
13	H	H	+6	H
7,7	H	+4	0	+4
8,8	Split	Split	+2	Split

This playing strategy covers every possible situation. It may not be perfect, but it has earned me over 2 percent of total dollars wagered. With it I win an average of six times every seven plays (45-minute sessions). Remember, this is a *playing* strategy, not a *betting* strategy, so I modify my betting count (Table 2) for aces before deciding how to play a given hand. To maximize my advantage, I only play against single or double decks. At the time of this writing I am still allowed to play in every Nevada casino and I have never found it necessary to play against four decks, which decrease player expectation. This strategy is adequate against four decks but not ideal.*

* For further sophistication against four decks, I recommend either of the two previously mentioned systems with playing strategies (see page 18).

4

Some Good News
and Some Bad News

My first trip to Las Vegas was ten years ago. I had just finished graduate school, with its consequent impoverishment. Hungry for money, of which I had seen precious little for the past five years, I bought a copy of *Beat the Dealer* by Dr. Edward Thorp. Having struggled through Thorp's "10-count" blackjack system, I played several hundred hands with my girl friend and was ready to tackle the Las Vegas casinos.

Las Vegas was much as I imagined it—expensive, gaudy superstructures on barren desert terrain. The entire scene had a surrealistic, Kafkaesque feeling. Enormous neon signs, fountains, and swank hotels in the midst of 120° desert heat and sandstorms. Inside these luxurious hotels an even stranger scene awaited. People, scurrying everywhere, seemingly dazzled by the glitter of the hundreds of chandeliers, were throwing away their money. Women in furs (outside, the heat would bring a desert Bedouin to his knees) were clutching paper cups filled with nickels and were playing three or four slot machines simultaneously. They would run to one machine, drop in several nickels, pull the handle, then run to the next before even observing the result; then to the next; then they would return to the first machine, taking a furtive feel of the payoff slot to see if any coins had been shaken loose, then repeat this bizarre dance. All the while, they were warily surveying "their" machines to forestall the approach of a possible intruder.

From the crap table came a demoniacal shriek—"YO-LEVEN—front line winner—pay the line. Place your bets now—they're comin' out—come bets, field bets, here they come. Four, the point—point is four; who wants the hard way? Five dollars on the hard way —take the odds. Here they come—" "*Little Joe*" one of the players squealed. Then cheers from around the table as the roller made his point. I was stunned and bewildered by this gibberish. Everywhere I looked people were in the same frenzied state—roulette, the wheel of fortune, keno, chuck-a-luck, baccarat; each had its frenzied addicts.

And then—the twenty-one tables—rows of them, the target, each with a few lambs crouching on stools and muttering about their "bad luck." A more pensive mood prevailed in this sector of the casino as each player tried to decide whether to hit or stand—guessing, then second-guessing, then praying: "Be there, be there, baby." —"Oh, no! Not again—another twenty-one. Don't you dealers ever break?"

Slipping into an empty seat, I made my first bet at blackjack—and lost. I carefully watched the cards as they were played, counting the 10's. An advantageous situation arose—I increased my bet tenfold. "Incredible," I said to myself, "I've got blackjack." I won the next hand and the next. Then back to a small bet as the deck soured. After an hour, I had won five times my original buy-in. A swarthy pit boss in a silk suit and white alligator shoes approached. "Like a drink?" he purred. "No, thank you," I replied. My God, he was watching me! Did he know I was counting? He stood very close and stared. The deck got rich again. I bet $100. The pit boss coughed—the dealer immediately shuffled the cards. I took my bet back and started again at $10.

Every time I increased my bet, the pit boss coughed; each time he coughed, the dealer shuffled. When the deck favored the house and I had a $10 bet riding, the dealer would continue to deal until he ran out of cards. But each time I increased my bet, I heard that doomsday cough and winced as the dealer shuffled. By some miracle I continued to win. I had played nearly two hours and now had almost eight times my original investment. Suddenly the ominous pit boss loomed again. This time the silky voice was replaced by a chilling knifelike quality. "We don't want to see you in here any more—cash in your chips and leave. Oh, and one more thing—don't come back!" Feeling someone's presence on my other side, I glanced up. A uniformed brute was staring down at me. I smiled; he didn't. Quietly I collected my chips and accepted the security guard's escort—first to the cashier, then to the door. I had been barred from my first casino after playing only two hours! I had won, but could no longer play at this casino. I walked out feeling dejected, even though I had won. I could see that longevity was going to be a problem.

* * *

First Aid to the Rescue

On to the next casino. Happy to have won at my first play, I was also perplexed and unsettled at having been barred. Starting to play again, my mind was still wandering. A good situation arose; I bet ten units. The dealer started to deal, then blanched. Beads of perspiration appeared on his forehead; then he fell onto the table scattering chips everywhere. Having been trained by the Boy Scouts in emergency first aid, I quickly pulled him off the table and onto the casino floor. He was about fifty and had all the classic signs of a heart attack. I told the head pit boss to call an ambulance. A few minutes later the dealer left the casino, bound for a local hospital. A casino executive was called. He thanked me warmly for what I had done and graciously informed me that my room and meal charges would be complimentary for as long as I cared to stay. The pit bosses were extremly cordial. I began to play again. I won steadily for three straight days. No one seemed to be paying too much attention and it seemed as though I had died and gone to heaven.

On the morning of the fourth day, coming down to the casino to play, I felt a perceptible change in attitude. As soon as I sat down, a covey of pit bosses arrived at my table. Although still cordial, they were watching me intensely. As play continued, they whispered furtively to one another. I had a particularly good run of cards and an enormous stack of chips. The atmosphere became increasingly tense. A crowd, attracted by my winnings, had gathered at the table. In retrospect, I should have quit. But I didn't, not when I had the bit in my teeth.

Then the incredible happened. With seventeen cards left in the deck, twelve were 10-value cards. The player advantage with this combination exceeds ten percent. I played two hands at $250 each. The dealer turned up a 6 for himself. I breathed a sigh of relief. My advantage had just soared to over seventy-five percent. He was now a strong favorite to break on this hand. I looked at my first hand—a 6 and a 2—a total of eight. I thought for a moment. In Las Vegas the player can double down on *any* two cards. Twelve cards were still 10-value cards and only two cards were not. The chances of the dealer breaking were enormous. The worried pit bosses were now practically in my lap. I showed them the hand. "What would you do with this?" I asked. "You've got to hit," the head pit boss replied. I said, "I know I have to hit, but with the luck I've been having maybe I should double down." He shrugged, "I wouldn't, but it's your money." "If you wouldn't, then it must be the right play," I said, smiling. I doubled down and was given a card. I peeked at it and was not surprised to see a 10. I now had 18. I moved on to the next hand. I quickly looked at the cards and was startled at what I saw—a 3 and a 2. Although only adding up to 5, these were the last two cards that were not 10-value cards. This meant that the dealer had to have 16 and would have to draw a 10, which would give him 26—a bust. My chances of winning were now a hundred percent. I couldn't lose! I turned to the pit boss and jocularly asked, "What would you do with this?" "Don't tell me you are thinking of doubling down on 5?" he said with a disgusted look on his face. "Yes," I said. "The way he's been running, I think he [the dealer] might break." I doubled my bet to $500 and was given a card—a 10, of course. The dealer turned over a 10, drew a second 10, giving him 26 as anticipated. He paid me $1,000 and started to sort the cards in preparation for shuffling. The head pit boss stopped him. "Wait a minute," he snapped. He took the eight unplayed cards and spread them face up on the table—all 10-value cards. He paused, then turned to me and said, "Friend, you're too tough. Please stay as our guest as long as you like, but no more twenty-one. Okay?" Without argument I collected my chips and cashed them in. I had played for four days and had a handsome profit, but the result was the same—I was barred from a second major casino.

A Casino Makes Me a Deal I Can't Refuse

After a two-day rest, I was ready for more action. At about 4:00 A.M. I ventured into another large casino. I like playing in the early-morning hours when the crowds thin out and tables are relatively empty. I played for a couple of hours and managed a small profit. From nowhere a pit boss appeared. "That will be all! We don't want any counters in here!" This time I protested. My win was a pittance and I resented being ejected again. A heated debate followed. Finally a casino executive approached. He was a small man with white hair and a booming voice. "What's the problem here?" he roared. The pit boss told him I was counting and said that the probabilities favored my continuing to win. "Probabilities, hell! Deal three hands and shuffle; let him bet anything he wants." The pit boss reluctantly complied. I changed my betting tactics. When the deck favored the house, I bet $25; when it favored me, I bet $500. This extreme increase in bet size would more than compensate for the fact that they shuffled after every three hands. Despite my advantage I seemed to lose nearly every $500 bet. After an hour I was losing $5,000.

The executive with the loud voice returned—"How are you doing?" "I haven't won a hand since you left," I complained. "Good," he boomed. "Now get lost, you bum—you had your chance." I was incredulous. "What do you mean?" "I mean you're through—get out of here!" I could hardly believe my ears. I had been soundly beaten and now I was being evicted. I swallowed my anger and slunk away.

The Fast Shuffle

I walked across the street, still fuming. I started to play again. This time I was greeted by a new casino tactic. Every time I increased the size of my bet, the dealer would shuffle. Since the system I was using required increasing the bet size under advantageous circumstances, the net effect of shuffling was to wash out all such situations. Frustrated, I changed my betting tactics. On the initial hand I bet three units instead of one. If the deck was favorable, I continued to bet three units. If the deck soured, I *increased* to ten units. The dealer would obligingly shuffle. This new strategy was working out splendidly. I was winning again and felt renewed confidence. Once more an observant pit boss intervened. Within an hour I was back on the street, again an exile.

Adding Insult to Injury

Being a slow learner, the morning found me in yet another casino. I fell behind on the first hand and continued losing at a rapid pace. After two hours I was losing over $7,000. The pit bosses were extremely cordial, commiserating with my ill luck. With considerable affectation, they would shake their heads in disbelief as I lost hand after hand. Then the cards suddenly changed. I started winning at a precipitous rate. Within fifteen minutes I recovered half my loss. When I bet $500 on two hands and got blackjack on both, the pit bosses' smiles faded. The head pit boss hurried for the phone. Within minutes a neatly dressed casino employee appeared. He was quiet, friendly, and thoughtful. He watched me play. Ten minutes elapsed and I lost $1,000. I was now $4,000 behind. The suave floor man approached me. "We would rather you didn't play here any more," he whispered. "But I'm losing a fortune," "I know, and we intend to keep it. Thank you for coming. Can I buy you a drink before you leave?" This was becoming a recurring nightmare. I had been in Las Vegas only ten days and I was already running out of places to play.

Planning a New Strategy

The story was the same everywhere. Although the amount of time differed, the result was invariable. I was either evicted from the casino or the dealer was instructed to shuffle after *every* hand until I left voluntarily. At one casino I was asked not to play before I even sat down. I had been fingered by a fink down the street, who gratuitously provided my description. I was barred on sight. My system was just too easy to detect. Tired and depressed, I decided it was time to leave Las Vegas and develop a new, more sophisticated strategy. I did not return for six years. (For the record, I have since been allowed to return to all of the casinos that evicted me.)

5

How Not to Be
a Counter

After my first visit to Las Vegas, I spent a great deal of time reflecting on the experience. Gradually, insights for a winning strategy began to emerge. It became apparent that much more than just the play of the cards was involved. Playing and betting strategies are very good as far as they go. What dawned on me was that no one had delineated a total "strategy" for plundering the Las Vegas casinos. I started with the inescapable premise that counters are considered undesirable by the casinos (to put it mildly). This being true, it becomes important not to act like a counter. This led to an intricate strategy of camouflaging my play, controlling my emotions, swallowing my ego, and adopting a demeanor diametrically opposed to the mechanical style of the typical counter. With a new image and identity I was soon to return to Las Vegas.

What describes the counter? From my own extensive observation and from the accounts of several seasoned Las Vegas casino executives a list (Table 8) of "counter" characteristics emerges and an adjacent list of preferred characteristics for the winning player also becomes apparent.

TABLE 8

Typical Counter Behavior	Preferred Behavior
1. Intense concentration	1. Acting unconcerned
2. Acting guilty and suspicious	2. Making eye contact; be natural
3. Sneaking in and out of casinos	3. Acting confident, looking at ease
4. Walking up and down inspecting tables	4. Walking directly to desired seat
5. Deliberate betting pattern	5. Irregular betting pattern
6. Stacking chips perfectly	6. Handling chips clumsily
7. Adding to bet at last moment	7. Thinking *before* you bet; bet early, never change a bet once made
8. Avoiding interaction with floor personnel	8. Inviting interaction with floor personnel
9. Making good plays that seem bad, to avoid suspicion	9. Making truly bad plays to avoid suspicion
10. Acting like computers —methodical, calculating	10. Free and easy style
11. Looking like a professional card hustler	11. Looking like a tourist
12. Playing long hours	12. Playing 45-minute sessions

When the counter first enters a casino he is wary. He walks up and down the aisle surveying the tables and pit bosses. He wonders if anyone will recognize him and throw him out. After finding the table he wants, he will often stand behind it, carefully watching the dealer and the players. To maximize his advantage, he will sometimes wait until the deck strongly favors the player, then make a huge bet. His demeanor at the table is one of utmost concentration. Meticulously, he watches each card as he counts. If the pace of the game is slow, he will study the cards again, just to be absolutely certain he hasn't erred in his count.

His betting is deliberate, calculated. He handles his chips in a polished manner and stacks them in neatly organized, regular piles. Fearful that the dealer will shuffle the cards in a favorable situation, the counter will often wait until the last possible moment to place his bet, then quickly make a big bet just before receiving his cards. This often agitates, if not angers, the dealer. When approached by a pit boss, the counter withdraws into his shell. He acts as though he is doing something illegal, arousing the suspicion of the pit boss. He avoids eye contact and begins to fidget. Many idiosyncrasies become apparent as his anxiety increases. The counter may begin to play with his chips, smooth his hair, or scratch his nose.

One young counter would constantly adjust his glasses, wrinkle up his nose and squint whenever approached by casino personnel. His face was so contorted it looked as though he had some horrible affliction. A pit boss actually asked him what was wrong with his face. He answered lamely, "Oh nothing—it runs in the family." The pit boss laughed and scrutinized his play even more closely. After several minutes the young counter could no longer stand the pressure and scurried away from the table as if he had been wounded. The pit boss turned to a colleague and asked if he had ever seen this kid before. He acknowledged that he had seen him on several occasions. "Keep an eye on him if he comes back," the first pit boss said, "I think he's doing something. He sure looks suspicious." This story ended with the counter being barred from playing.

Another counter was being watched by a very knowledgeable casino representative. The player wanted to deceive the houseman, but was loath to give up anything in the process. He assumed he could make a lucrative play that would appear absurd. The count got to plus 7, with a little over a quarter of the deck remaining. He was dealt two 10-value cards and the dealer showed a 3. A large bet was at stake. The player looked up at the pit boss and smiled weakly; then split the two 10's. He was given an ace on the first and a 10 on the second for totals of 21 and 20 respectively. The dealer's down card was a 10 and he drew a 10 for a total of 23—a bust. As the player was collecting his winnings, the casino man came over and began whispering in his ear. Moments later the counter was escorted from the casino.

Bad plays for purposes of deception can be very useful, but they should be genuinely poor plays. The play in the second example was actually correct, and very sophisticated. Assuming a knowledgeable person is watching, a *truly* bad play may throw the watcher off the track. You may actually convince him that you are a poor player. The winning player should not be afraid to sacrifice a little at the right time to create a "proper" impression. One of my favorites is splitting 3's against a 10 with a small bet at risk. This play is most unusual and will be viewed as a sucker play.

Often, a counter will play for long hours, grinding out his victories. One would actually bring a bag lunch, then play incessantly, snacking at intervals to quiet his hunger. Fried chicken was his favorite food and the greasy dripping and strong odor would discourage others from playing at his table, thus increasing his win rate. He would play for ten to twelve hours at a time, between bites of chicken, without changing expression. He can no longer play twenty-one in Nevada.

It is important not to fall into behavior patterns that characterize counters. You can only be a counter if you don't *seem* like one. Be as relaxed and casual as possible. Walk directly to the seat of your choice and sit down. Immediately engage the dealer in conversation. Phrases like "How have you been running?" or "Did you just start working?" break the ice. Make eye contact, smile and be pleasant. Small talk and cordiality are disarming. It is important to get the dealer to like you. He can be a great ally if he so chooses. You must not antagonize him. A constant stream of patter is helpful. Home towns, length of time in Nevada, family, sports, investments, and world events are useful topics of discussion. It is helpful to make a bet for the dealer soon after you sit down. Never tip a dealer directly. Instead, add to your bet what you would normally tip, clearly telling him that you are betting it for him. Now he wins with you and loses with you. The bulk of a dealer's earnings comes from such "tips," so this early gesture lets him know that you can be a rich source. (See chapter on Dealers.) When a pit boss approaches, look up and greet him. Introduce yourself and shake hands with him. Continue to play, making small bets, while you engage him in conversation. Talk with him for as long as he wants. Don't handle your chips efficiently. It is preferable to appear awkward, especially in the presence of a pit boss. Consult him frequently on the play of difficult hands. Give him the impression that he is the expert. When he gives you advice, tend to follow it even if it's wrong (especially when small amounts are involved).

In short, it is paramount to behave in a nonchalant, natural manner to avoid suspicion. If you feel comfortable within yourself, this attitude will be detected by the casino personnel and they will react favorably. By establishing rapport with as many casino people as possible, you will be able to play for many hours without incident.

6

Camouflage

How to Emulate the High Roller

Having made a favorable overall impression and established an initial image, the next step involves your attitude while playing. I spent many hours observing players gambling for large stakes and noticed a number of common traits that could easily be imitated. The casino caters to the "high roller." This type of player is capable of losing tens of thousands, so the casino management bends over backward to make his stay as pleasurable as possible. The high roller will usually chat with the pit bosses as he plays. When drawing a fortunate card, he will show his hand to the pit, followed by a soft whistle or some other gesture of good luck. When the cards turn, he shakes his head in disbelief, crying, "I don't believe it; have you ever seen anything like this before?" At this, the casino floor men maintain somber façades, shaking their heads, clucking sympathetically—"Boy, you're really running bad. Hang in there, things will change." A communication loop is set up between player and house men. The player vents his frustration to an attentive, understanding audience.

The casino provides the support the player needs to dissipate his anger and frustration so that he will continue playing.

The last thing the house wants is a player quitting in disgust: in that case he may run off to another casino to lose his money. If the high holler starts to become superstitious—and this occurs frequently—the management will move to allay these fears: "Would you like a new deck? John, get me a blue deck, maybe that will help." If the player demands a shuffle, the pit boss will give the dealer a nod of approval, and the cards will be mixed.

I have found it immensely rewarding to pattern my playing behavior on this style. The more closely I imitate the high roller, the easier it is for me to win without being suspect.

Dress

Dress sharply. You should look as if you can afford to lose. For evening play, high-style suits or sports jackets are appropriate; during the day, well-designed casual attire is acceptable. I prefer coat and tie for both. Wear jackets that have readily accessible pockets, so that you can easily slip chips into them. (See chapter on Money Management.) Dress carefully, be well-groomed and clean-shaven, especially if you are under thirty-five. Young people betting large amounts of money are particularly subject to close scrutiny. If you wear jeans and a work shirt, have a beard and shoulder-length hair, the house immediately suspects you of counting. I saw two hip-looking men in their mid-twenties enter a Las Vegas casino and ask for three thousand dollars' worth of chips each. They requested a private table. The management refused. They played anyway. The dealer was instructed to shuffle every other hand. The house men camped at their table, closely studying the play. They played atrociously and within an hour lost their entire stake. They were not counters, but had they been counters, they would never have had a chance. Their age and appearance was all the casino needed to take every available precaution. I find it helpful to be extremely well-groomed, manicured, and dressed to the teeth so that my appearance is congruent with the size of my bets. It's like wearing a uniform to work, and high style is emblematic of the high roller.

Attitude toward Money

High rollers have a very nonchalant attitude toward money. I saw one big player bet $2,500 on a hand. He doubled down and now had $5,000 riding. At that moment an extremely well-endowed young woman sashayed past. The player turned and followed her with his eyes. The dealer broke and paid him. The player was oblivious to the transaction. For a full two minutes he continued to watch the girl, muttering softly under his breath. When his wits finally returned, he looked down at the table and smiled briefly at his huge mound of chips. He casually pulled three piles toward him, leaving $2,500 for the next hand, and continued to glance behind him, hoping for another glimpse of the woman. Compared with his lust, the money had little meaning.

This image of monetary insouciance should become part of your act. When a pit boss approaches and a large bet has been made, chat with him about some inconsequential topic. Then play the hand in a perfunctory manner, looking as uninvolved as possible.

Continue an unbroken stream of conversation as the hand is concluded. Whether you win or lose, appear emotionally uninvolved with the outcome. Nonchalantly gather your chips and place your next bet, all the while seeming enthralled with this idle chatter.

Tip liberally and irrationally. Make it seem as if you are just throwing away your money. As an illustration, a counter friend of mine had just finished a session with a handsome win. Ready to leave, he noticed he had stacks of $100 and $25 chips, and a lone $5 chip. He bet the $5 chip. The dealer directed his attention to the $25 minimum bet sign on the table. My friend said, "This five-dollar bet is for me, I'm betting twenty-five dollars for you." He then placed a $25 chip adjacent to the $5 chip. He won. He gave the dealer the $50, took the $10 for himself, and left. The pit bosses shook their heads in disbelief at the apparent disregard for the value of money. It was a brilliant ruse, and bought him thousands of dollars of additional playing time.

I like to appear to throw money around. When a security guard is controlling the gallery, which frequently is attracted to big play, I will toss him a $5 chip for his services. The same principle applies to cocktail waitresses. After they bring a drink to the table, I'll wait until they start to leave, then flip a $5 chip on their tray.

One day an elderly janitor was watching me play. He kept milling around my table, rooting for me. I added a $5 chip to my bet and told the dealer that this was for the janitor. I also bet an additional $5 for the dealer and several hundred for myself. I was dealt a 12 and the dealer had a 10 up. Turning to the janitor, I asked for counsel. He said, "Lord only knows, boss; just play it the best you can." Next, I looked at the dealer and showed him the hand. He quietly said, "You're not dead yet." I interpreted this to mean that he had a small card in the hole. I stood. The dealer turned over a 6 and drew a 10 for a total of 26. The only way I could have won the hand was to stand on 12, with the dealer showing a 10. Both the dealer and the janitor had also won their bets. As I gave them their money, I noticed the dealer giving the janitor a subtle wink. "Praise the Lord," the janitor said as he trundled off with his $10 gift. I made several other bets for this janitor during my various trips to this casino. I was especially prone to bet for him when the management was watching. This type of behavior is most atypical of counters.

Playing the Cards

Look as if you are having a good time when you are winning. Most counters never change their facial expressions, win or lose, but the high roller is excited when winning. Be enthusiastic and lively at the table. I often ask the dealer for certain cards. Once I was dealt the 6 of clubs and the 8 of hearts. With a pit boss standing next to me, I said to the dealer, "Now will you please give me the 7 of spades to go between these two." Like a genie obeying my command, she turned over the spade 7. The pit boss stared in disbelief, and the dealer murmured a few words of apology to her startled superior. Without changing facial expression I said, "Thank you very much. That was very thoughtful of you." The pit boss laughed at my mock sincerity and ambled off to watch another game.

On numerous occasions a card-calling contest has developed between the pit boss and me, with the dealer caught in the middle. The more superstitious the pit boss, the more heated these affairs became. On one occasion I had 18 with a very large bet riding. The dealer had an 8 up. I knew there were three 9's left in the deck. "I stand," I said, "have a nine." The pit boss countered, "Don't you dare have a nine, have a three." Obligingly, the dealer turned over a 3. "Now little," I cried. Before the pit boss could say anything, the dealer turned up an ace. She now had a total of 12. "Now a nine," urged the pit boss. "No! Little again," I pleaded. She turned over another ace. "Now the nine," I shrieked. "No nines," yelled the pit boss. The next card out was the 9 of clubs, breaking the dealer. "No!" the pit boss moaned, "don't listen to him. I want you to listen only to me. Understand?" This interchange was all done half in jest, with good-natured teasing on both sides. From my standpoint, it served as a wonderful distraction. The pit boss became so involved in the battle of wills, he paid no attention to my betting or the play of the hands. We could have gone on for hours without his noticing that I was counting.

Superstition

The degree of superstition of some pit bosses is truly amazing. A friend of mine related a story that happened several years ago. A high roller in craps was playing at one of the Strip hotels. The pit boss on the game was an old-timer named Squatty Cohen. The player was winning consistently. A break-in dealer was on the game. As the player continued to win, Squatty muttered to the dealer, "Hit the end of the table with the dice." The dealer said to the player, "Sir, would you please throw the dice a little harder." The player responded by throwing the dice more powerfully—another winner. "Hit the end of the table with the dice," grumbled Squatty. The dealer said, "I'm sorry, sir, but you'll have to throw the dice harder." This time the annoyed player threw the dice very hard. They flew across the table, hit the far wall, ricocheted wildly, flew back across the entire length of the table, and landed in front of the player. "Seven, winner seven," called the dealer.

The young dealer was replaced. Cohen took him aside and admonished him, "I told you to hit the end of the table with the dice." The perplexed dealer said that he had told the man to throw the dice harder on several occasions, and that the player had practically knocked the table over, he was throwing so hard. "That's not what I mean," snapped Squatty. "I mean, when you give the dice back to someone that's running good, you should hit the end of the table with them. That shakes em' up and ruins his run, see?" "Sure," said the wide-eyed dealer, "anything you say, Squatty." Cohen's attention returned to the game, and finally he could stand it no longer. The player was still winning, and just before he was about to throw the dice again, Squatty rushed forward and said, "Wait a minute!" He then proceeded to draw a double X with his fingers in front of the startled player. With a sneer he said, "There, that ought to take care of this nonsense." The player never made the next roll. Angrily he snatched up his winnings and stomped out, never to return to that casino.

A similar incident happened to me in blackjack. One evening, while playing alone at the table, I was winning steadily. The pit boss kept changing decks—four times in thirty minutes. When this didn't work, he took out a matchbook and set it up on the counter. He opened the cover and exposed three matches without breaking them off. He then bent one of the matches and pointed it at me. I continued to win. He bent a second match and pointed it at me. Still, I won. Finally, with a smirk, he bent the third match and pointed it at me. I lost the next hand. My forty-five minutes of playing time had expired, so I left. I'm sure he thinks his jinx drove me away.

At another casino a short, bald, pugnacious-looking pit boss paced up and down in front of me while I was winning. I continued to win and he disappeared. He returned shortly, wearing a flaming crimson tie. Standing a short distance away, hands on hips, he glared at me with his tie fully exposed. I assume that the tie was supposed to unnerve me and make me lose. *

Voodoo such as this is reasonably common in gambling circles. Since superstition is so rampant, it can be turned to your advantage. Sometimes, when the deck is bad, I will ask the dealer to shuffle, especially if he has just won a number of hands in succession: "Shuffle and start over—let's start fresh, you've won enough hands in a row," I will say. They will usually comply. Or I will ask for a new deck at an opportune time. Let's say, on the first hand after a fresh shuffle, I'm dealt two 10's, and the dealer has a natural 21. The count is now minus 5. At this juncture I might say, "That does it—I can't even win with 20—let's have a new deck." It's important not to abuse this ploy, but rather to use it sporadically when you are losing. Remember, when behind, you can get away with more by acting superstitiously.

You can also demand a change of dealers. In one instance, I was playing against a dealer who dealt less than

* In ethnology it is commonplace that male animals attempt to intimidate their opponents by a display of certain brightly colored anatomical parts.

half the cards, then shuffled. I was losing and wanted better playing conditions. Rather than ask him to deal farther down at the risk of creating suspicion, I called over the head floor man and asked him to put Robert at my table. I had played with Robert before, and knew that he dealt down to the last eight cards or so. The pit boss said he could not do that. I decided to call his bluff: "Then I won't play until I can play with Robert," I said. "I'm not going to continue getting butchered. I really like Paul here, but I can't win two hands in a row and I want a new face." Convinced that I was motivated by superstition, the pit boss told Paul to change tables with Robert. With the improved playing conditions, I quickly overcame the deficit and managed a substantial win. I thanked the pit boss for accommodating me, emphasizing how Robert had changed my luck.

Superstition can be a good excuse for increasing the size of your bet. At a Lake Tahoe casino I bet $25 off the top of the deck. I lost. Again I bet $25 and lost. The count had now jumped to plus 4. "Let's change the order of the cards," I said, and played two hands, betting $50 on each. I had used superstition as an excuse for increasing my bet four-fold.

Although acting superstitiously can be effective camouflage, it is imperative that you not succumb to superstitious ideas. I know a number of proficient counters who have been greatly distracted by an unfortunate series of events. One was convinced that his luck was bad in a particular casino, or, worse yet, that he had been cheated. Paranoia running wild, he thought that a certain dealer wearing sunglasses looked particularly suspect. He proceeded to lose six consecutive hands with large bets at stake. He was now convinced that this dealer had been brought in for the express purpose of cheating him. On another occasion, this same man thought the house would send a shill to play at his table and take his cards whenever the deck was rich. He became so agitated and distracted that his concentration was impaired, and he lost a great deal of money in a very short time. Worst suspicions confirmed, he refused to play again in this lucrative casino.

Don't let yourself fall into this trap. If you play long enough, amazing sequences of events will occur purely by chance. I have lost twenty-two consecutive hands. Another time, in eight hours of play, I was dealt only four blackjacks. During the same period of time the dealers received thirty-six blackjacks. I have had a dealer go through eight straight decks without breaking. I have experienced a dealer getting all four aces for seven decks in succession. All this, and more, happens at random, and you must not let it effect your play.

Playing with Female Partners

High rollers are often accompanied by one or more women. Female companions lend support and gratify the ego. In such situations, it is common for the woman to pick up the cards for luck or even to play a hand for her escort. Women can be a tremendous aid to the male counter, but they must have the proper personality and disposition for the task. I find it impossible to play effectively if there is any emotional discord. Your female companion must clearly understand what your goal is and what her role is in its attainment. She must not hassle you. Her function is to distract the casino personnel. The more effective her distraction, the less likely you are to be noticed. Your playing companions should be beautiful and glamorous. Striking women attract immediate attention from the bored floor men. They should be extroverts and flirts. One woman I play with fits this bill par excellence. She is five feet ten, with long blond hair freely falling to her waist. Her perfect tanned face is beautifully complemented by emerald green eyes. Her voice has a throaty purring quality. She knows exactly how to excite the ever-randy bosses. Within minutes, she would have them so "turned on" they couldn't see my cards had they been looking (which they hadn't). Once I glanced up and saw no less than five pit bosses with their eyes riveted on Britt. She met their gaze evenly with a seductive smile. During the many hours I have played with this lady, I have never felt any casino pressure.

Women can also be useful in the play of the cards. In good situations, I like to play more than one hand. House rules dictate that the first hand must be played before you can even look at the second hand. Sometimes the cards contained in the second hand can influence your decisions on the first hand. When playing with a woman, she can "play" the first hand while you play the second. You can then look at both hands simultaneously. By tapping her with your knee beneath the table, you can give signals on how to play the hand. I use one tap for stand, two taps for hit, three taps for doubling, and four taps for splitting pairs. This allows me the advantage of seeing both hands. It also provides the added camouflage of having a woman play hands for large stakes.

Interaction with the Gallery

When playing for high stakes, there's often a crowd of observers. These people, from all over the country, get vicarious excitement from seeing big money change hands so quickly. They almost always identify with the player. Some actively root for you, as they would for their favorite boxer. I have found it useful to play up to this fancy. I pick my cards up so that they are in clear view. In tense situations, I will often slowly "squeeze" the cards to intensify the drama. Casino floor personnel will frequently get caught up in this bit of suspense. With craned necks they too will anxiously wait as the cards gradually become visible. Once again this provides a misdirection of attention.

The gallery will often give advice. One session I played attracted a particularly large audience. A very outspoken, handsome southern gentleman was standing at my right shoulder. For half an hour he had been giving me constant encouragement. The count got to plus 8, with half a deck remaining. I had a $400 bet. The dealer showed an 8. I was dealt a 6 and a 4. "You've gotta double," my southern friend boomed. I took his advice but did not look at the card that was dealt to me face down. The dealer turned over a 3 and hit it with a 10, giving him a perfect hand—21. "We're in trouble now," I said to my pal. Ever so slowly I peeked at the card I had been given. When I saw what it was, I prolonged the drama, finally turning over an ace. I had tied the dealer's 21. My erstwhile friend shrieked with glee. "Leave it all out there," he screamed. "After a break like that you just gotta bet it all." Since I had doubled down the hand before, I now had $800 in the square in front of me. Normally I would have taken half of this back. I looked up at the pit boss. "He's been givin' ya good advice so far," he said. I turned to my right and said, "Okay, I hope you know what you're doing." With the count still at plus 8, I was delighted with an excuse to bet the extra amount. I placed the two cards I was dealt neatly together, one on top of the other. Then I turned the cards over, revealing an ace. "You're halfway there," the gentleman drawled, "c'mon baby, be there!" Slowly I squeezed out the spade jack. My friend gave out a whoop, befitting a brahma bull rider, and shouted, "See, didn't I tell ya—there was never a doubt." I thanked him profusely and he ran off to tell his friends about his great adventure. Bless his hide.

Theatrics

I have on occasion experimented with acting out various other roles. Once I portrayed a drunk. I really got into the feeling of being polluted. My speech became slurred, my thought process slowed, and I was having difficulty remaining steady on the stool. Several times I knocked over my chips. My head began to swim, and I lost steadily. This act ended when I made a large bet late in the deck on the assumption that an ace remained, and was appalled to discover that all four had already been played.

I still use one ruse of this type. I frequently go to bed early in the evening and get up at about 6:00 A.M. Donning an evening suit, I begin to play. "Been up all night?" the pit boss asks. "Yeah," I say, "I've lost everywhere else, so I thought I'd try here before giving up." Floor men are used to people staying up literally days on end to gamble, so this story is readily accepted.

Their guard lowered, it is easy to make a forty-five-minute play without attracting any attention. The same routine can be repeated at several casinos in the course of a morning.

Use Your Own Style

For you who intend to try these ideas in practice, it is important to grasp the underlying principles and adapt them to your unique style. You must feel comfortable at the tables. You must also be exquisitely aware of the ambience and react in a manner that minimizes suspicion. Understanding the behavior pattern of the typical player will enable you to modify your play within the framework of your own personality, thus making the best of your winning potential.

7

Money Management

Successful gamblers manage their money skillfully. If you were to approach a professional gambler and offer him five times everything he had on a flip of a coin, he would refuse. Even though the odds are five to one in his favor, he would not risk everything on a one-time proposition. He has learned how to make his living based on thousands of trials in which the odds favor him, and he carefully controls the money he risks on each trial.

Playing to Get Even

The discipline of prudent money management will provide you with big dividends—if adhered to rigorously. Most gamblers tend to lose control when behind. They play more and more carelessly and bet their money progressively more freely in an attempt to recoup their losses. Playing to get even can have devastating consequences. Good counters are particularly vulnerable to this pitfall. Because they know they are overwhelming favorites to win, they tend to take liberties, with disastrous results for both the short and long terms. When behind, they may bet twice their maximum, with only a slight advantage. They would not dream of doing this when winning.

I have observed superb counters start with a comfortable $50 unit. Their bets will vary from $50 to $200. An adverse run of cards then sets them back $1,500. At this point the good money manager will quit, accepting his loss and maintaining his self-control. He knows that each session is independent of the last and wants time to settle himself before returning to play. But a preponderance of good players refuse to accept a momentary defeat. They feel frustrated and angry. Beads of perspiration dot their foreheads. Faces are flushed, palms sweaty. This reaction obviously affects their playing ability. Instead of betting $50 to $200, they bet $100 to $400—and more. The more they lose, the more they bet. The play of the hands cannot possibly be as accurate under these physiological and emotional circumstances. As they continue to lose, they begin to feel sick. Now, behind $5,000, despair starts to mix with their mounting anger. They press further, playing two hands at $500 each. The confidence they once had is shattered, and they expect to be beaten hand after hand. They feel fortunate to win with a 20. The impossible is anticipated, and it occurs. The dealers seem to make incredible draws, and the players sink deeper into the morass of uncertainty and despair. Then they begin to punish themselves for this idiotic display of emotionalism.

Losing all concern for the value of money, they virtually throw it away. Their betting pace becomes frenetic, with ensuing astronomical losses. In this state, they will continue to play until their entire bankroll has been squandered. Eight hours and $20,000 are down the tubes. Dejected and exhausted, they collapse into bed and agonize over what went wrong.

It may take months to overcome such a crushing defeat. It takes its toll not only on the player's finances, but on his psyche. As new wins are ground out, there is a slow return of confidence. For some players, a session like this marks the end of their playing career. If you are to be a winning player, you must not be caught in this trap. It blinds you to your surroundings. You will no longer care what the pit bosses are thinking, and you will be stripped of your camouflage. I have watched counters who have lost control and blown horrendous amounts of money; then regain composure, only to be barred. The observant floor man waited until the momentum turned, then asked the player to leave. The counter vociferously voiced his displeasure, reminding the executive of his $10,000 loss. Unmoved, the pit boss replied that he was quite aware of how much he had lost, but was also onto his act. The casino intended to keep his money and was not inclined in the slightest to give him a chance to win it back; not then, not ever! Here we have the worst of all possible worlds—a large monetary loss and eternal exile from the premises. And it is all so needless—this set of circumstances should never have occurred.

How to Bet Your Money

Your betting pattern should appear natural, but you must subtly control it. Most high rollers will "parlay" their money. When they win a bet, they will "let it ride," sometimes until their bet reaches the house limit. In a recent newspaper article, Mike Goodman, manager of the new Marina Hotel in Las Vegas, stated that "the strength of gambling is to bet more when you are winning, not when you are losing. That is the secret of gambling." This statement is clearly fallacious and self-serving. The house will win a fixed percentage of the total dollars wagered, and the player can only lose in the long run. This common notion of betting more when winning can, however, admirably serve the counter.

Never increase the size of your bet above two units unless you have won the preceding hand. In this way, you camouflage your betting strategy by making your increase look like a parlay. Of course, you only parlay when the count indicates a bet increase. For example, you bet two units off the top of the deck. With Las Vegas rules and a proper basic strategy, you are even money to win this hand. If you win, and the count is plus, let your bet ride. Four units are now at stake. If you win again, you might add a fifth unit if the count remains positive. If you lose, however, cut back to your original bet of two units, no matter how rich the deck may be. Increase your bet again only if you win and the count warrants it. If the count turns negative, decrease your bet to one unit. So long as the count is minus, continue to risk only one unit, whether you won or lost the preceding hand. At a count of zero, bet two units. It is important to vary your betting strategy so that it does not appear methodical.

Both Thorp and Revere recommend very structured betting systems. Thorp advocates betting one unit for each plus in your count, regardless of the outcome of the previous hand. With a count of plus 7, bet seven units; if the count then drops to plus 4, bet four units. All minus counts dictate a one-unit bet. Revere recommends a parlay system not to exceed four units. With this system your bets will be either one, two, or four units, depending on the count. Revere also rightly recommends not increasing your bet unless you have just won the hand.

I think both these systems are too structured. It is sometimes preferable to bet three units in good decks, sometimes five. Also, alter the number of hands you play. Spreading out to two hands allows you to bet more, without a conspicuous mound of chips. When you play two hands at three units each you are, in effect, betting six units. Sometimes, if you are being closely watched, play two hands at one unit each when the deck is slightly minus. If the deck then turns positive, and you have won on either hand, you can leave the two-unit bet untouched and make a second bet of one or two units. The main idea is to bet more when the count is favorable and less when the count is adverse, but you have great flexibility within this framework. Creativity along these lines will help prevent detection. But remember always to maintain control. Don't press and don't unduly increase your bets when you are losing. Try to make your betting decisions quickly and smoothly. Avoid measuring your bets and appearing to ponder each decision.

Try not to change your bet when the dealer shuffles. Late in the deck, limit your bet to two or three units. If the dealer shuffles, just leave it alone. You have just as much chance of winning the first hand of a new deck as he has. Large bets near the end of the deck may scare a dealer into shuffling, even though you arrive at the larger amount by parlaying. Since your advantage is greatest late in the deck, you want to delay shuffling as long as possible. So don't get greedy!

There will be times when the situation will demand

changing the amount of your bet. This is particularly
true after a tie hand, a "push." In these instances, the
dealer will leave your bet untouched. Let's say the count
is plus 2, and you have bet four units. Both you and
the dealer are now dealt two card 20's. The count is now
at least minus 2, and you do not want to have four
units riding on the next hand. This calls for some diplo-
macy. I like to say, "I always cut back after a push,"
or "If I can't win with a 20, I'd better cut back." Then
I reduce my bet to one unit.

Controlling the Size of Your Wins and Losses

Keep the size of your wins and losses down. Don't
win or lose more than twenty-five units. This may happen within ten minutes. If so, quit. One of the nice
things about playing twenty-one is that you can always
find a game, at any hour. There is no harm in retiring
after a short session. By keeping your wins and losses
small, you will avoid attention. One day while I was
playing, a pit boss whom I had come to know especially
well approached me and asked how I was doing. "I'm
winning a little," I said. "You don't stand a chance at
this game," he said, "you never bet enough when you're
winning." "You're right," I said, "I guess I just don't
have the heart for it." "Yeah," he sighed, "you don't
play that bad, but you never win enough to amount to
anything." I was extremely pleased by this conversation. The truth is that I had won more at this casino
than at any other, but my small wins were hardly notice-
able.

Concealing the Size of Your Win

Several techniques are available for concealing the amount you win. Pocketing chips without being noticed is effective and easily learned. Pit personnel will keep track of the money you spend buying chips. The dealer will call over a floor man every time he makes change for you. The floor man keeps a running total of each player's investment. When you leave, he will estimate how many chips you carry away and convert this to dollars. The floor man turns in a tally sheet on each player that looks like this:

PLAYER NAME	BUY-IN	WIN/[LOSS]	WALK	RATING
Ian Andersen	$500	[$200]	$300	1

The buy-in column records the total amount of cash exchanged for chips. The win/[loss] is the result of the play. Losses are bracketed. The walk column indicates the amount of chips the player has when he leaves the table. The rating describes how good or bad a player is for the house.* By pocketing chips, you can appear to lose while actually winning. In the above example, I really won $400, yet the pit recorded a loss of $200. During the course of the session I pocketed $600 in chips. I had been playing at a $25-minimum table, and

---

* Casinos rate players from one to four. A one is a high roller—a player who bets his money fast and should be given V.I.P. treatment. A two is a good player for the house, who bets moderate amounts. Threes are still smaller players who risk very little. Category four contains undesirable players, such as cheaters, thieves, and counters.

several players had come and gone. I had many opportunities to inconspicuously remove $25 chips. Upon leaving, I grumbled mildly about my $200 loss and left with only $300 in visible chips.

Only redeem the amount of chips you appear to have when you leave the table. Some casinos have feedback between the cashier and the pit. If suspicious, the pit boss will call the cashier's cage and ask for a report on how many chips you cashed in. Have a friend cash in the chips you pocketed, or, if no one is available, redeem them later.

Another method of concealing gains is to change tables. The pit boss must keep a record of your performance at each table. His task is complicated when you hop from table to table. Often he will merely be guessing. If you drop a few chips in your pocket as you move, his chore becomes extremely difficult. Don't overdo this, however, because pit bosses will begin to resent you. I like to move when it seems natural, as when I have been losing consistently or have given back a large percentage of a win.

How Long to Play

Play for forty-five minutes or twenty-five units, whichever occurs first. You need to discipline yourself not to play longer than forty-five-minute sessions. Playing winning blackjack is hard work, and you need to have all your faculties alert. The closer you adhere to this principle, the better off you will be. For one thing, it is difficult for even a competent pit boss to be sure you are a winning player in this short period of time. Many players count something, but few are skilled enough to win. An observant pit boss may think you are one of the many who know just enough to lose.

Short playing periods will protect you from big losses. Remember, you should never risk more than twenty-five units in one session.

After a forty-five-minute play, take a break even if you still feel fresh. Clearing your mind and relaxing for as little as fifteen minutes has a very beneficial effect. You will be surprised at the difference this makes. Alert and refreshed, you will return with renewed vigor. Some of my best sessions have occurred immediately following such a break.

About six sessions in twenty-four hours is maximum. I find myself patterning my day around plays. A usual day will include getting up at about 6:00 A.M. and making a play; then eating breakfast and putting in a second session. Next, I like to spend several hours in the sun, culminating in a long swim—then back to the tables. After a mid-afternoon nap and shower, play again. Following this, a relaxing sauna, whirlpool, cold bath, and massage, dress for dinner, then a fifth session. Play a final round after dinner, then go to bed.

When to Play

I am often asked what time it is best to play. When playing for high stakes, most casinos will make room for you at any hour. With smaller stakes, quiet casino hours are best: 5:00 A.M.–10:00 A.M., 4:30 P.M.–6:30 P.M., 8:00 P.M.–10:00 P.M. By 5:00 A.M. most people have collapsed, and few awaken prior to 10:00 A.M. From 4:30 in the afternoon to 6:30, guests are napping or preparing for dinner; and from 8 to 10 in the evening they are either eating or attending a dinner show. Another excellent time to play is at the end of a shift. This has two advantages. First, the pit crew is tired and their concentration worsens near the end of the work day. Their thoughts filled with the idea of going home, or of evening plans, they tend to study their watches instead of your play. Second, most casinos do an accounting an hour before the next shift takes over. All results during this final hour accrue to the next shift, so if you win a bundle, they couldn't care less—the loss will reflect on the next shift. Often competition exists between shifts, so they may even relish taking a loss during the last hour.

There are about thirty casinos in Las Vegas. Each has three shifts and each shift is virtually autonomous. So in any given twenty-four-hour period there are ninety possible sites to work. By moving around and playing six sessions a day, you could play for two solid weeks without duplicating shifts.

It is acceptable—in fact, expected—for you to play proportionately more at the hotel at which you are staying. This is convenient but should not be abused. It is often difficult to overcome the inertia to stay in one place. Overplaying a casino can create needless problems and should be avoided. Besides, moving around has the advantage of a new stimulating environment and a different set of playing conditions to help sharpen your acuity.

I frequently check into several hotels simultaneously. It's good not to overplay one casino, so I like to spread myself around a bit. Since it is awkward to repetitively play at places which I'm not staying, I oblige the local customs, register, and take a room. I travel with several sets of toiletries, and evenly distribute my togs among the various facilities. This widens the choice of gourmet restaurants and gives me alternative pads in which to crash, as well as the needed camouflage. Usually I register under a pseudonym—protection against one hotel checking with another, unearthing my little ploy.

Fringe Benefits

The fringe benefits of being a desirable customer are enormous. I rack up over $30,000 yearly in free hotel bills, eating like a gourmand, and drinking nothing but the finest—Dom Perignon, 1966, or Château Lafite Rothschild, 1959. Oh yes, the casinos pull out all the stops for their esteemed guests. My air fares are covered, and my guests and I are quartered in palatial suites, with mirrors everywhere (Las Vegas is big on mirrors). Expensive, if not tasteful, the rooms are done in early Sodom and Gomorrah style, with gold carpets and red drapes trimmed with purple to complement the ubiquitous reflections. It's like an adult Alice in Wonderland and sometimes I have difficulty believing all this is really happening. After being pampered by such lavish accommodations, they allow me to win thousands. The mind boggles!

Keeping a Diary

It is a useful discipline to keep a diary. Include the date, place, and time of play, the length of the session, the amount won and lost, and noteworthy events that transpired (see diagram). This will supply you with data on how much you have played at each casino and the result. From this record you can calculate your hourly compensation and evaluate your play. You should win about eight to ten units per hour. The column on comments will refresh your memory on important events prior to your next play at a given casino.

A close friend of mine has devised a scheme to bypass the sensitive issue of pit-boss interaction and playing times. He keeps a master journal of all Las Vegas casinos. He plays for no more than an hour a day, and only plays against shoes (4 decks). He makes small bets and waits for a good shoe. If a shoe turns in the player's favor, it tends to remain lucrative throughout. When this happens, my friend starts betting wildly, increasing his bet size from $25 to $500, or even $1,000. He only plays out the one shoe. Then, win or lose, he leaves. The startled pit bosses have no chance to evaluate his eccentric betting pattern. He logs the time and date of his visit and the result. Methodically he plays on each shift at every casino before repeating the circuit. In this way he has averaged $50,000 per year for the past three years and has never felt any casino pressure!

Making the Best of Playing Conditions

Never play with more than one other player at the table! More players than this dilute the favorable situations. The dealer will also tend to shuffle sooner to insure against running out of cards. This means that there will be times when you will not be able to play. Resist the temptation to play anyway. After a while the tables will clear, and you will have your opportunity. If conditions change in the middle of a session, leave immediately. Don't even stop to consider whether you are ahead or behind. Since you need every possible edge, you must adhere strictly to this rule.

When approaching an empty table, sit in the middle

SAMPLE DIARY ENTRY

CASINO	DATE	TIME	WIN/ [LOSS]	UNIT SIZE	COMMENTS
Sands Hotel	6/15/75	7:00 –7:30 A.M.	+$250	$15	*Pit boss named Jake closely watched play. Dealer named Mike dealt almost all the way down. Casino almost empty—played alone most of the time. All the tables used four decks.*

seat. If another person wants to play, he must now sit on either side of you. This enables you to see his cards and add them to your count.

If another player joins you in the middle of a rich deck, feel free to ask him politely to wait until the dealer shuffles. Tell him that you are superstitious and have a good run going, and don't want him to change the order of the cards. Most people will gladly accommodate you.

When you are playing for high stakes, other players will often ask if you would rather play alone. Don't be shy. Thank them for their courtesy and concede that you really would prefer a private game. The only exception to this rule is if you know the other player and are aware that it will be advantageous for him to join you. Some players provide such effective distractions that you will be unnoticed by comparison. One such player is a middle-aged Oriental gentleman named Lee. He is a dramatic player. Lee loves to play blackjack and plays for high stakes. He puts incredible energy and concentration into every hand. He feels that, by using all his brain power, he can influence the cards. When he draws, the casino gives the dealers special instructions to deal the card face down. Lee will then lift the card off the table without looking at it and weigh it in his hand. If the dealer shows a 10 and Lee is drawing to 16, he will concentrate intensely as he weighs his "hit" card in the palm of his hand. After careful consideration his head will nod slightly and he will say, "Light—this card is very light. I think, maybe, a four. No, heavier than four, maybe five." When Lee doubles down with 11, he will weigh the card and say, "Oh! Heavy; very heavy—feels like a big, fat king." It is a delight to play with Lee. His antics completely distract the floor men, and since he is a consistent loser, they cater to him. He adds levity to the game. When the two of us are playing together, we look like two idiots throwing money around in sheer delight. When I double down on a big bet, I will ask Lee to "weigh" the card dealt to me. For some reason, he tends to be more accurate in his predictions of my cards. With Lee's "help" I win steadily; he is an excellent diversion.

Another player who is wonderful to play with is Marty. He is a heavy-set, gray-haired, boisterous man from the East. He plays so badly and loses so much that the casinos allow him to take excessive liberties. When he has finished acting on his hand, he will lean over the table and look at the dealer's hole card. I sit a couple of seats to his left. Although he tries not to reveal what he has seen, his facial expressions frequently give him away. I base my play on Marty's unknowing signals. Sometimes I stand on 12 against a 10, and other times I hit soft 19 against a 10. I never do anything so gross as to hit hard 17 or 18, even when I knew this is proper, because many casinos now have a standing rule that the dealer must call over a pit boss if a player draws to hard 17 or higher. This play is so unusual that it usually means the player is either cheating or being tipped off to the dealer's hole card. (See chapter on Cheating.) Marty loses so much that it makes my small wins seem inconsequential. The casino never says a word to either of us.

Another V.I.P. player with an amazingly advantageous playing trait is Edna. She is an extremely affable, elderly woman of means who makes frequent trips to Las Vegas just to play twenty-one. She has tremendous stamina and can play for ten to twelve consecutive hours. She bets $100 on every hand. Edna's quirk is that she insists the cards be dealt until the dealer runs out. If the house won't grant this demand, she refuses to play. Since she is likely to lose a small fortune each trip, the house accommodates her. Playing with Edna and counting is like being in heaven. The added advantage of seeing fifty-one cards each deck is enormous. When a new dealer comes on and shuffles early, I gently point this out to Edna. Outraged, she will chide, "Young man, at this table you deal until you run out of cards." The dealer will argue that the rules don't allow him to do this. "What rules?" Edna snaps. "Call over your boss there, and he'll tell you about rules." The dealer will call the pit boss, who will tell him it is all right to deal out all the cards. My best trips have been when Edna is in town.

Controlling the Limit of the Game

As you become an accomplished blackjack player, you will want to play for progressively higher stakes. On every blackjack table there is a sign indicating the minimum and maximum bet. The higher the minimum bet, the fewer the number of players. Minimum bets can vary from 50¢ to $100. Two dollars, $5, $25, and $100 are the most common minimums. The successful counter wants to play in a game with a high minimum. This prevents small play and limits the number of players. Often it allows the counter to play alone.

The best time to raise the minimum on a game is before you start to play. If you know the casino personnel, this is an easy task. Ask them what size game *they* want. If they suggest too small a minimum, ask if they want you to just play around or really gamble. They will get the message and find the sign you want.

Sometimes they will hustle you into a higher-limit game. At a casino in downtown Las Vegas, I bought in for $500 in quarter ($25) chips. After playing for a while they began paying me with $100 chips. Before I knew it, I was out of quarter chips. I turned to the pit boss and asked what he was trying to do. Candidly he said, "You've got hundreds; play for hundreds!" "You're really hungry," I said, smiling. "I'm already losing, and now you want to go for the jugular." The pit boss laughed but made no move to give me change. "Okay," I said, "I guess I'll just lose it a little faster. Give me a hundred-dollar sign." The pit boss responded immediately. I played for forty-five minutes, won $2,000, and left, thanking the pit boss for making it all possible.

At times your request for a higher limit will be rebuffed. I have seen high rollers become temperamental at such times, with good results. Having tried this myself on several occasions, it works. A good example of this happened at Lake Tahoe. I was playing alone at a $5-minimum table, and asked the pit boss to change it to a $25 minimum. He politely refused. I was losing about $400 and had $100 bet, when a birdlike little man with a pince-nez on his beak placed five Eisenhower dollars in the betting square next to me. I had 19 and the dealer showed a 6. The new arrival peaked over his nose pincher at a pair of deuces. He looked at me briefly and chirped, "I'm not going to draw and take his card." He stood. The dealer turned over a 10 and hit it with a 5, for a total of 21. With a sheepish smile the little man slipped away. I acted incensed. Fortunately, the pit boss had observed the entire incident. "That's it for me," I said, putting on my superstitious hat. "Did you see that? He stood on four. That's the only way I could have lost that hand. If he split them, or just hit, I would have won; but to stand, that's hard to believe! I'm not going to let anything like that happen again. I'll just take my five-hundred-dollar loss and go, unless you make this a twenty-five dollar game." The pit boss finally relented. He could see my point, and I really seemed annoyed. He did not want to lose me.

If you are not granted a higher game at first, try again later, especially if you are behind. Casinos tend to be a little more pliant when they are ahead. Their initial fear is replaced by greed, and they will eagerly reverse their decision if given a graceful out.

Unit Size and Your Bankroll

To decide what size unit to use, first establish the amount of capital you intend to risk. Divide this amount by 125. The quotient is your unit size. For example, if your total bankroll is $250, your unit size should be $2; if your bankroll is $6,250, then your unit size should be $50. As previously discussed, only risk twenty-five units at each play (one-fifth your total bankroll). This formula will minimize your chance of ruin. The chances are better than nineteen out of twenty that you will not lose your bankroll before the odds swing your way. As your bankroll expands, slowly increase your unit size.

Don't bet money you cannot afford to lose. People who play on tight money don't play well. The pressure is too great; the fear of loss will inevitably affect your play. Blackjack should be looked at like any other high-risk investment. Only risk capital should be committed for play. Start slowly. Time is on your side. The casinos are not going anywhere.

How to Handle Losses

The true test of a winning gambler is not how he handles winning, but rather how he reacts to losing. There are times when you are going to lose. Prepare yourself for these occasions. It is imperative that you maintain emotional self-control at all times. Take a long break after a loss. Relax and regain confidence before playing again; you need to be psychologically prepared for your next play. Remember, each play is unrelated to the last. Treat each as a separate entity; don't contaminate a fresh play with memories of a recent loss. Learn to handle losing; winning will take care of itself.

Using Casino Credit

All Las Vegas casinos, and most of the other Nevada casinos, do an enormous amount of credit business. Credit-worthy customers are given a limit for each visit. This functions like a revolving charge account similar to BankAmericard, except there is no interest or finance charge. Say your limit is $5,000 and you lose it. Your credit is now exhausted. If you repay $2,000, you now have $2,000 of credit again. For most players, their debit balance is in a constant state of flux. They lose, pay off some of their balance, lose some more, then pay some more. For this reason the casinos have millions of dollars of accounts receivable outstanding. Terms for repayment of gambling debts can be established, and some large losses are paid off over long periods. A central credit bureau exists to provide casinos with quick credit information on known players.

Mr. W. has a $10,000 card (credit limit) at the Sahara Hotel. Then he decides to stay at the Sands Hotel. He applies for credit. The Sands checks with the central bureau and finds out that Mr. W. has an active $10,000 card at the Sahara since 1970. There have been no collection problems. Within twenty-four hours his credit is granted at the Sands. The hotel is motivated to do this since it would like to have Mr. W. as a regular customer. To this end it matches his existing credit limit.

I strongly recommend counters establish credit at several prominent casinos. This is standard procedure for big players. Playing with cash is suspect, much as is using cash for large purchases. Like the rest of the world, Las Vegas thrives on its credit business, so do the natural thing and use it.

There are many advantages to using credit as well as a few drawbacks. We have already discussed one of the main advantages—camouflage. Credit fits in with the profile of a high roller. Another merit of using credit is that it gives the casinos a reading on your activity. Casinos like fast players—a fast player bets his money aggressively and is apt to sustain large losses. They also cater to players who make frequent visits. Both of these activities are monitored by the credit department. The credit slips (markers) you sign are recorded daily on your card. Any casino executive can look at a card and quickly evaluate the player. An example of a typical card is depicted in Table 9. From this card it is readily apparent that Mr. Brown is a desirable player. He comes to town about three times a year and plays for high stakes. His debts are paid promptly. Because of his activity and payment record, his credit limit is increased to $15,000. It looks as if Mr. Brown loses about $20,000 a year. He is highly regarded by the casino and given V.I.P. treatment, including complimentary room, food, shows, and transportation. Actually, Mr. Brown is an expert counter. He uses casino credit to create the impression that he is a big loser. Using the money extended to him by the casino to pay off his markers, he pockets his blackjack winnings. He successfully uses casino credit to seem like a loser, and disguises his true activities.

Once you have established credit at one casino, it is easy to secure it at another. Set up numerous accounts and stay at different casinos. By so doing, you can play at many casinos without arousing suspicion.

TABLE 9

Name:	John Brown
Address:	7 Boulder Dr. Chicago, Illinois
Tel. No.:	(312) 652-0000 (home)
	(312) 379-0000 (business)
Occupation:	Real Estate Broker

DATE	DEBITS	CREDITS	BALANCE
2/14/74	$4,000		$4,000
2/15/74	3,000		7,000
2/16/74	2,500		9,500
2/17/74		$9,500 (check)	–0–
9/5/74	5,000		5,000
9/6/74		2,000 (chips)	3,000
9/7/74	7,000		10,000
9/8/74	3,000		13,000
9/15/74		10,000 (check)	3,000
1/19/75	4,000	7,000 (cash)	–0–

DATE	CREDIT LIMIT	BANK REFERENCE
2/14/74	$10,000	Name of Bank–Continental Illinois
9/6/74	15,000	

Address–Chicago, Ill.

Officer–Mr. Murphy

Type of Acct.–Checking, Business

Bank Credit Checks:
2/14/70 Mid 5 figure Checking Acct.

Excellent rating by bank.

COMMENTS–Will pay off markers at our Chicago office.

Using casino credit can also help your cash flow. Thirty-day settlement terms are common and casinos will readily accept postdated checks. So for short periods of time you can have the use of the casino's money. This should not be overdone, and debts should be paid promptly so as not to jeopardize your status.

The main disadvantage of using credit is that you must use your own name. Communication between casinos is uncommonly good. If you have been banned from playing at one establishment, there is a high probability that word will spread. One casino may call another, flagging your card and noting your activities. The next time you come in and ask for credit, the pit is alerted and you are barred.

A second disadvantage is that it is easier for the pit to track your wins and losses when you use markers. These credit slips give them an accurate fix on how many chips they have issued to you. It is more difficult to determine precisely the amount of chips a player has purchased when he uses cash. Money is immediately dropped down a slot in the table into a locked box. There is no record of the amount, other than whatever notation a pit boss may make. If the casino is busy, you can dupe the average floor man into believing you have lost more than you actually have. Make small frequent purchases of chips. Check with the pit boss periodically to find out where you stand. On one occasion I had bought $2,300 in chips. I had purchased odd amounts —$600, $700, $300, $700. On some hands I bet money instead of chips. In this manner I had lost an additional $300. I called a pit boss to the table and asked, "Where do I stand?" He said, "I think you're in twenty-five hundred." I said, "I know it's more than that; it's at least three thousand. Did you see the last seven hundred?" He confessed that he had not. "That explains it," I said. "With that I'm in thirty-two hundred." The pit boss nodded, made a notation on his pad, and moved on. When I checked with him subsequently on the amount I was losing, he was right on target—"my" target. This deception would have been impossible had I been playing with markers. The written record would have revealed the true amount of my chip purchases and enabled the house to ascertain more accurately the result of my play.

Where to Keep Your Money

Whenever you have a sizable win, the casino representative in the cashier's cage will ask if you want a receipt for it. He takes the money and holds it in safe-keeping until your departure. Don't fall into this trap. These deposits are closely watched, and a record of them is released to all areas of the casino. Some casinos have computers that contain this information, as well as your credit limit and current balance. Each area of the casino has a terminal and can quickly discover the amount of money you have on deposit. To avoid this, keep all your money in your own safe-deposit box. All the Strip hotels have safe-deposit boxes available for their guests, but many of the hotels attempt to discourage their use. Insist on having one. It will make discovery much more difficult for management.

At times, even a safe-deposit box is not adequate precaution. I had a $25,000 credit limit at a large Lake Tahoe casino. Over a period of time I walked off with the full $25,000 in chips, plus my twenty-one winnings. The casino records showed me owing $25,000, making payments of $5,000–$10,000, then losing again to bring my debt back to $25,000. Everything had gone smoothly for several years—I had gradually increased my credit limit from $5,000 to $25,000, while averaging $15,000 in yearly profits.

Then one day an unexpected complication arose. I arrived for a scheduled one-week stay. This time I decided to reduce my outstanding debt from $25,000 to $5,000. I paid the credit manager $20,000 in cash. I had brought an additional $10,000 with me and tucked it away in a safe-deposit box. During the next four days, I gradually redeemed $20,000 worth of chips, signing markers and siphoning the chips out of play. In addition, I won $12,000 in that four-day span. My box now swelled with $42,000 in cash—the $10,000 I had brought, the $20,000 I had removed from play, and my $12,000 win. The credit manager, a little gnome-like man in his late sixties, had been in gambling his whole life. He took me aside and asked why I was always at my credit limit. "That's quite simple," I responded, "I lose!" "Well, take it easy," he retorted. "Bring it down a little every now and then and don't lose it back right away." "I'll try," I said, "but it's hard to quit a loser when there's more credit available." "I know, I know," he clucked, "but try, okay?"

I returned to the casino to play, slightly unnerved by this wily old veteran. I wondered how much he really knew about my activities. If he only knew what was in the box. . . . The next hour provided little to allay my mounting anxiety; the little gnome was cagily observing me. Several times I got a glimpse of him cruising the twenty-one tables at which I was playing. He showed up at a nearby booth while I was having lunch. When he miraculously materialized at an adjacent urinal in the men's room, I started to come unglued. I wanted to get that money out of there—and fast. Several hours passed. A friend agreed to watch the cashier area and tell me when the coast was clear. Finally he called to inform me that my opportunity was at hand. I sidled up to the cashier's cage and presented my key to the clerk. No one else was in sight. The clerk obligingly handed me my box. Then it happened—the glint of an elderly blue eye from behind the filing cabinets. Zap! From out of thin air my elfin-like tormentor had returned. Now what? Thinking fast, I whipped out the remaining few hundred dollars in my pocket, opened a hairline crack at the top of the box, forced the bills through the small opening, and clamped it shut tightly. The old man sauntered over to me. "What's in the box?" "Jewelry, a little cash," I answered. "You through with it?" he questioned. "Yeah." As he picked it up, I could see his experienced, almost childlike little arms weighing and measuring the contents. God! What if he opens it? As luck would have it, he didn't want to chance this invasion of privacy. He returned the box to its place and reluctantly returned the key. "Jewelry," he muttered under his breath.

I continued my vigil well into the night, keeping tabs on the old coot. At 4:00 A.M. sleep finally overtook him. Once again I crept up to the cashier's cage. I breathed a sigh of relief to see an old friend on duty. Quickly I emptied the box of its contents, slipping my cuff links, gold bracelet, and watch in its place. Returning the box, I rushed to the casino across the street, safely depositing the $42,000 in a new box. With a sigh of relief I returned to my hotel and retired. Next morning I found my nemesis once again hawking me. Now, however, I moved with assurance. Boldly I walked up to the cage and asked for my box. He arrived at my side just in time for the grand opening—watch, bracelet, cuff links, and a few hundred dollars I had deposited the previous afternoon. The game of cat and mouse was over and I had narrowly escaped.

Having learned my lesson, I now take additional precautions, especially when sporting large amounts of cash. I deposit my bankroll, winnings etc. in a safe-deposit box at a neutral casino. I make sure I don't play at the casino in which my cache is stored. This way, suspicion and detection are kept to a minimum.

8

The Casinos
Strike Back

The single greatest problem you will face as a counter is to be able to continue playing. Greatest jeopardy will stem from an inability to control your ego needs—power and status. First, you really must understand your objective. For many, this is much more than money. Power needs prevail. The monetary objective is contaminated with enhancement of self-image, at the expense of casino personnel. Some, obsessed with their "macho" image, "put down" the dealers and pit bosses. Due to strong status needs they want to "crush them" or "smash them." By putting others down, they engage in the futile attempt to raise their self-esteem. The money is symbolic of being stronger and more powerful than the casino. At the same time, however, they are afraid; they suspect that the casino men will pick up these "vibes" and retaliate. They are on enemy turf and are apprehensive about a counter-attack. They are notably lacking in openness, candor, and warmth. Hostility, defensiveness, and suspicion prevail. They are uptight, guarded, snide, and combative. Their hostility, however, is misplaced. Why are they angry at the casino? Although the casino had done nothing, it looms as a threat to power needs.

The books I have read on twenty-one seem to encourage competitive relationships with the house. In *Beat the Dealer*, Professor Thorp defies the casino to figure out what he's doing. He reports one instance in which a casino man thought he was identifying small flaws on the backs of the cards. When they carefully examined the backs of the deck, Dr. Thorp "scoffed" at them. Then he "pressed them" further, wanting to know what they thought of his "secret." The dealer responded by telling him they thought he could keep track of every card, betting and playing accordingly. Dr. Thorp bristled at this and "challenged the dealer," claiming that no one was capable of this feat. The dealer said the pit boss behind her could do it. Again Thorp responded aggressively by offering first $5, then $50, then $500 for a demonstration. When the casino did not respond, the professor left "in disgust," revolted by the behavior of these "sportsmen."

This is an excellent example of the type of behavior I think should be avoided. Dr. Thorp apparently needed to "put down" the casino employees. Throughout his book his motives are mixed. Strong power needs contaminate, if not totally eclipse, monetary gain.

In Lawrence Revere's book, *Blackjack as a Business*, he makes clear a total lack of respect for pit bosses. To sum up their competence he states it takes three pit bosses to change a light bulb—one of them to hold the bulb, and two of them to turn the one holding it. This contempt and total disregard must have been felt when Mr. Revere was playing. No one likes to be regarded as a fool, and response is likely to be severe.

A striking comparison exists between this behavior pattern and that of other animals. When a strange wolf enters another's territory, conflict arises. The local wolf defends his territory and attacks the intruder. So long as the invader remains combative, the battle persists. Increased aggression by the visitor is returned in kind. One of them must lose, and it is almost always the stranger. In a sudden gesture he rolls over, exposing his neck, and the battle ends.

This analogy approximates the typical casino–counter relationship. As soon as the floor man senses conflict, he reacts as though his territory is being threatened. Gradually he becomes enraged. He responds to the threat, reciprocating with aggressive behavior. This builds to a climax and the player is ultimately chased away. A game has been set up where someone must win and someone must lose—and guess who loses? The intruder is playing on the casino man's turf and will always be turned away. From this point on he is viewed as the enemy, and any future visits immediately incite rage in the casino representatives, their turf penetrated by a known aggressor. Seeing casino personnel as the enemy *makes* them the enemy, and they strike back. The extent of this vehemence can be truly awesome.

An acquaintance of mine, Mr. S, was attending a bridge tournament at a large Strip hotel in Las Vegas. He had been expelled from this establishment five years previously, ostensibly for counting. He had not played since. The bridge tournament featured a formal dinner in one of the large convention facilities. After dinner Mr. S was chatting with a group of six people, all attired in formal dress. They were standing against a wall at the far end of the casino, some fifty feet from the twenty-one pit. A man dressed in a business suit slowly walked past them, casually surveying the group. When his eyes fell on Mr. S, he did a double take, focused, and searched his memory for this familiar face. A flash of recognition filtered through his stare and he hurried away. Mr. S, aware that most major casinos have floating floor men who walk around like tourists to protect the casino from undesirable elements, sensed trouble. The floater scurried to the other end of the pit, approached the head pit boss, and began talking and pointing in an agitated manner: "That guy in the red velvet tuxedo—I know who he is—he's eighty-six! * We don't want him in here. Tell security I want him out—now!"

Mr. S, observing the frenetic gesturing and hostile glances, started for the exit. As he did so, the floater and head pit boss also started for the door, walking briskly between the two rows of blackjack tables. As they approached, they were joined by additional casino personnel. Two pit bosses and the casino manager fell into line. Three security guards and a second floater joined the swelling ranks. Mr. S, attempted to avoid a scene, quickened his pace. The casino men had now formed three lines bordering the twenty-one tables. When they saw that Mr. S was escaping, they started running after him. The casino manager shouted the player's name at the top of his lungs, demanding that he stop. A security guard intercepted Mr. S at the door. The casino manager shook a finger in his face and threatened: "Let's get one thing straight, buddy—you're not to play in here! If I see you in this casino again, I'll see to it that you won't feel like returning." All this

* 86 is a term used in casinos for people who have been permanently banished.

commotion had attracted a crowd of about fifteen people. Mr. S said, "I'm not playing and I don't intend to play—I'm here for the bridge tournament. You can check on that, if you like." "I don't care what you're here for. Get out and don't come back or I'll have you arrested for trespassing." One of the organizers of the tournament was observing this scene. He joined Mr. S and asked what was happening. Informed that Mr. S was not allowed to play twenty-one, he personally guaranteed no twenty-one would be played—only bridge.

During the three days of the tournament, my friend was under surveillance. All three shifts were brought into the game room to familiarize the pit bosses with Mr. S. The floaters were notified as well, and he was closely watched whenever he walked through the casino—an altogether unpleasant experience.

Another player had been barred from a large Strip casino in 1968. He returned five years later and deposited $20,000 in twenty-dollar bills as a playing stake, registering under a pseudonym. While his deposit was being counted and sorted, the casino manager recognized him. As soon as he left the cashier's window, the executive queried the head cashier about the transaction. He then called the local police, ordering a full-scale investigation. Four detectives with drawn guns broke into the player's room while he was sleeping. They searched his bed, suitcase, clothing, everything, without telling him what they were looking for. The FBI, Secret Service, and IRS were notified. They reviewed every $20 bill. The Secret Service checked for counterfeiting, the FBI for theft. They tried to trace the serial numbers. The IRS quickly probed the player's businesses, bank accounts, and tax returns. The detectives took him to the police station, photographed and fingerprinted him. The hotel bellman identified the player's car, and this, too, was searched.

The inquest revealed nothing. After six hours of torment, the player was released. The casino manager told him to pick up his money and leave—that his business wasn't wanted. Angry and frustrated, the counter requested his money from the cashier. In the interest of convenience and time (it takes a while to count out $20,000 in twenties), he asked for $100 bills. The cashier refused. She insisted on giving him his original bills. When he objected, she said coldly, "These or nothing." He acquiesced.

In retrospect, he thinks the casino manager was badgering him as punishment for counting. If the casino thought it had a chance to win the money, it would not have questioned the deposit, or at least it would have had the money investigated quietly. This idea was reinforced when the casino manager, without apology, asked him to leave after everything had checked out. He thinks the casinos have a strong influence on the judicial system in Nevada * and that this entire investigation was performed at the casino's request.

* Although a peripheral issue, the relationship between the casinos and the courts is of interest. The extent of this influence is still to be tested. A stockbroker was recently barred for counting at a Strip hotel. He was taken into a back room, questioned, expelled, and told not to return. He subsequently filed a $1,000,000 suit for harassment and prejudicial treatment. He had not cheated and yet had been forceably ejected from the premises. Knowledgeable people I have interviewed think the casino will win the decision at the Nevada hearing, but, if the case is appealed to a higher court, may have some exposure. The issue of the legality of barring people for counting is far from closed, and I would not be at all surprised if the rights of the counter were upheld in the federal courts.

I believe this is another example of territorial impingement. The casino, recognizing a known enemy, struck back. The player was not being punished for counting per se, but for the threat he posed to the casino's power.

How, then, do you avoid entering into a competitive relationship with the casino staff? You must clearly limit your objective. My sole motivation is greed—pure and simple. I have no desire to try to attain self-acceptance at the casino's expense or to usurp its power; I just want the treasure it guards. To accomplish this end, there is no need to put anyone down, prove my manhood, or gain glory. The wolf story contains a valuable lesson. As soon as the invading wolf turns his neck, the fight ends. So I turn my neck. I'm not trying to "beat" anyone. I'm using a system, and applying it objectively to obtain a specific reward—money. To do this I put the casino men "one up." They have all the knowledge and insights, and I prevail upon them to share their secrets. I humbly ask their help and they comply. This makes them feel good about themselves, raising *their* self-esteem. I treat them with regard and appreciation, making them feel they are persons of worth. Entering into a warm and dependent relationship, I listen to their problems and offer assistance wherever I can. In an open manner, I treat them with respect, while always down-playing my own abilities. Playing this game, everyone wins; the house man improves his self-esteem and I my balance sheet. By my becoming a welcome visitor rather than an intruder, they tend to pass over my monetary gain.

Minimize your risk and exposure. If a pit boss begins to seem suspicious, leave immediately. After playing for a while, you will begin to sense changes in attitude. Whispering between two pit bosses, their backs turned to your table, is a frequent early sign of trouble. Another is when the floor man assigned to your game leaves for a discussion with other pit bosses, the focus of attention obviously being your table. Depart in a calm, relaxed, casual fashion. If a person you do not know starts watching you, try to find out who he is. Introduce yourself and try to engage him in conversation. If he refuses to interact and seems hostile, remember an appointment for which you are late. Be unruffled, courteous, and friendly. Don't let your apprehension betray you.

If you are ever asked to leave, don't protest—depart promptly. Don't cash in your chips, just head straight for the door. Some casinos will try to photograph you. This can be done by a floater with a micro camera or from above.* Each casino keeps what it calls "the black book." This scrapbook contains pictures and descriptions of people who are "86." It includes cheaters, chip hustlers, bum-check men, counterfeiters, thieves, and other scam artists. (See chapter on Cheating.) One section is reserved for counters. It describes identifying characteristics, mannerisms, speech defects, tics, articles of jewelry, known disguises, aliases, etc.

The casinos have excellent intelligence systems. They remember names and faces for years. One counter spent $500 for a professional disguise. He went to a casino from which he had been barred five years before. As soon as he sat down, a floater approached and asked

---

* Every major casino has either a catwalk or cameras (called "the eye in the sky") stationed above every table. Both are used primarily to detect cheating but can also be used to study and photograph counters. Every game can be observed from above without arousing suspicion below.

him to leave. Amazed at the swiftness of detection, he asked how he had been recognized. "Your watch," he was told. "It's the only one like it I've ever seen."

Casinos must protect themselves from the myriad hustlers and thieves who attempt to part them from their money. In addition to floaters, employees are available to follow anyone who creates suspicion. They can uncover a person's identity, where he is staying, whom he may meet, and his automobile license-plate number. Next they check this data against the black book to get a handle on the suspect player. Often these investigations lead nowhere, but occasionally they uncover elaborate capers.

One ploy involved a group of five young counters. The first four occupied seats at separate twenty-one tables, where four decks were being dealt (four decks is commonly referred to as a "shoe"). They then counted the shoe at their respective tables, making $5 bets. The fifth player, a known man of some substance, had previously established $25,000 of credit. In an apparently random fashion, he wandered from table to table, making $1,000 bets. He was actually receiving signals from his four friends telling him when each shoe was ripe. Then he rushed over to whichever table favored the player, making maximum bets and trying to act like one of the crazy high rollers who often behave erratically. After a while he left the casino. Casino intelligence put a tail on him. Half an hour later, he and his friends met. The casino was given a full report, and their little game was over. Word spread through town and the other establishments were alerted. Central credit was contacted and the player's credit file was tagged with details of the ruse.

*   *   *

It is essential not to arouse suspicion. One potential pitfall is the way you handle losing. You need to swallow your pride, overcome your fears, and control feelings of anger when losing. Act as if you deserve it. After all, this is the expected result. Remember, everyone is *supposed* to lose, so lose graciously. Exaggerate losses and underplay gains. A loss is great public relations, so play it up to the hilt.

When I lose, I make sure everyone hears about it, especially if it is a significant amount. I ask the pit bosses what I did wrong, concluding that I play terribly. Many counters slink away after a defeat, angry and resentful. It seems to me they are blowing a golden opportunity. Recently I made a trip with a superb player to a casino in which we were both unknown. We stayed four days, guests of the hotel, and we both played for high stakes. As chance would have it, my friend lost consistently. After each losing session, he would rush away from the tables without a word to anyone, flooded with frustration and anger. His pride wounded, he threw caution to the winds and started betting wildly in favorable situations. As his hostility mounted, all he could think about was "crushing them." Eighteen thousand dollars went down the tubes during our four-day stay. Despite this enormous setback, the casino attitude toward him was, at best, lukewarm. The open hostility he had displayed had left its impact, and no one seemed pleased by his loss.

A loss like this could have very favorable consequences. If, instead of sulking, he had cried on the casino's shoulder, begging for advice and support, he would have been warmly received. The amount of his loss would have been indelibly inscribed in the formidable memory banks of each pit boss, and on future visits he would be eagerly welcomed by all. This could have been the platform for unlimited play. By keeping future wins small, they would look inconsequential. The casino would remember his big loss for many months (especially if appropriately reminded), and he would have had clear sailing for some time to come. But due to his strong ego needs and hostile manner, I doubt if he will ever be able to recoup.

When you win, let the casino know how fortunate you feel, not how smart you are. This is one of the most valuable lessons I learned from my early experiences. No one, least of all casino personnel, likes to be shown up or played for a chump. Perhaps you recall my describing early in the book a situation in which I doubled down on 3–2 when a dealer showed a 6, and all the remaining cards were 10's. That was my last hand at the casino. The casino manager looked at the rest of the cards, saw they were all 10's, and threw me out. Had I not been so clever, I might not have been hassled. For the most part it doesn't pay to make a highly unusual or brilliant play. This is usually done more for ego aggrandizement than for loot.

So be humble. Swallow your pride and subdue your power needs. Remember, the meek shall inherit the earth.

9

The Twenty-one Dealer:
A $10,000-a-Year Gift

An Ear for a Dollar

Yearly, dealers are worth a minimum of $10,000, *if handled properly*. If you make them feel good about themselves and help them enjoy their work, they will reciprocate generously by making the treasure they guard more accessible. If they choose, dealers can help you or make your life miserable. They are often surprisingly autonomous and make their own decisions about whether to deal or shuffle. Since the second half of the deck is particularly lucrative for the counter, the dealer can greatly influence his win rate. He can shuffle, erasing a juicy deck, or he can continue to deal far beyond the point he would deal normally, increasing your profit potential.

So how, then, can you persuade the dealer to bend a little in your direction? Again, good interpersonal relations do the trick—respect, friendship, communcation, and reward. Make the dealer feel wanted, a special person, not merely an automaton endlessly dealing cards. By its very nature his job is boring. Just imagine being on your feet eight hours a day and continually shuffling and dealing cards. Some of these people have been doing this for fifteen years! When ennui overtakes them and they no longer give a damn, it is easy to understand why they vent their spleen at the slightest irritant. It's your job to provide them with a moment of pleasure, to break up the tedium. If you can lighten their load by showing a little interest, they will respond. Some reciprocate immediately, others warm more slowly, but nearly all will eventually come around if you find the key that allows you to break the ice and make personal contact.

I treat the dealer respectfully, acting politely and with compassion. I find out his (or her) name and remember it. Each time I return, I make a special effort to greet the dealers I know. I ask about their health, family, hobbies, interests, and remark on changes in their weight (if they have lost), hair style, nails, or jewelry. Being as observant and attentive as I can, I listen to their stories and problems, gaining their confidence and becoming their friend. As our relationship grows, they gradually open up and communicate more sensitive issues. Like most of us, they need someone to listen to them and in the gambling community find precious few. By listening to their problems, I often supply the feedback they need to solve their own problems. I try to grasp and reflect their underlying feelings—boredom, frustration, anger. They may speak of repulsion for a superior or suspicion toward a player. I avoid being critical or judging these feelings; instead, I try to "feel" my way into the dealer's position and "grok" his emotions without judging him. I don't give advice, only reflect on what I hear and observe.

A good example of this occurred on my last trip to

Las Vegas. A young, competent dealer had just been chastised by a pit boss for making a minor mistake. He turned to me and said, "That guy is going to drive me to drink. I can't stand him, can you?" Rather than answer his question, I said, "You're feeling angry at the way he talked to you, is that it?" "Yeah," he said, "he always seems to make a mountain out of a molehill, and it really gets to me. How do you think I should handle him?" "I don't know," I replied. "You think he blows things out of proportion and this gripes you, is that right?" "Exactly," he replied, and breathed a long sigh, his expression visibly changed. "Well, let's deal you a few winners," he said after a moment's pause. Strange as it may seem, this simple formula of paraphrasing and clarifying feelings works remarkably well. By knowing he had been understood, the dealer felt much better and attributed his improved state of mind to our relationship. He would deal out *all* the cards (unless I asked him to shuffle). With knowledge of the remaining cards, this gave me an enormous edge and I won a bundle.

Loosening Up the Dealer

The secret is to create a situation in which the dealer wants you to win and puts all his energies into helping you. I try to make the game pleasant and interesting, eliminating the pressures that normally surround big-money games. Most dealers are nervous when they start at a table with big bucks. They know that if they lose, the floor men may blame them for the loss. The tension can be so thick, you can cut it with a knife. I've seen dealers afraid to smile for fear of repercussions from a superior. Lighten up the atmosphere! I will start clowning with their superior, drawing him into some inane, funny conversation. After a while we will both be roaring, and the still terrified dealer will vouchsafe a small smile. As time passes, it appears obvious that I have little or no concern for money, I'm just having a good time, laughing whether I'm winning or losing. The tension evaporates and the dealer makes some primitive attempts at conversation. Unpunished by his bosses, he continues to open up. He gradually realizes that this is somehow different from other big games he has dealt. No one seems concerned—neither the pit bosses nor the player—so why should he be uptight? More and more he falls into the rhythm and finds a refreshing interlude from his daily routine.

Help

Dealers enjoy this atmosphere and often ask to deal at my table. Once, two young dealers made a $50 bet as to which could "pump me up" with money fastest. Each dealt for forty minutes and did everything possible to lose. One lost $2,200, the other $2,700. Jubilant, the winner liberally thanked me for helping him win his bet. The loser was only mildly dejected, as I had placed a number of winning bets for him during his stint. That night, in the bar, the three of us laughed about some of the antics during those wild two hours. Both of them had consistently "tipped off" their hole cards. The first leaned forward every time he had to draw. (When the dealer has a 10 up he has to peek to see if he has an ace in the hole for blackjack. He now knows his exact hand. If he has a 2, 3, 4, 5, or 6 in the hole, he has a high probability of losing *unless* I break first.) So when I had a bad hand (12–16), I would show it to the dealers and watch their reaction. When the first dealer would lean forward, I would stand, knowing he was likely to break. The second dealer was less subtle. When he had a bad card, he would start to reach for his cards before I signaled whether I would hit or stand. When I noticed this gesture, I would promptly place my cards beneath my bet and stand; he would then have to draw, and usually broke.

The competition was close. The second dealer knew I had already won $2,200 from the first dealer. Time was waning and I was ahead only $1,700. On the dealer's final hand the deck was loaded. I had two $500 bets riding. As he saw his replacement approaching, the dealer dealt rapidly. To this day I don't know what happened. With lightning speed he whipped out the cards. He turned up a 10 for himself and, while I was still perusing my hands, quickly turned up his hole card, a 4, and hit himself with a 10, going bust and winning his $50 bet (not to mention my two $500 bets). I never made a move on that hand, never indicated whether I wanted to hit or stand. He was acting exclusively on his own. He even seemed to know he would draw a 10 to his 14. When I asked him about it over drinks that evening, his nose wrinkled up in a smile and he said, "I had to win my bet, didn't I?" and shrugged. I knew that was all he was going to say, but it was clear he had "peeked" at the top card and, knowing it was a 10, proceeded to hit himself before I could screw up the hand, costing him his bet. (See chapter on Cheating.)

Unsolicited help of this type has been common in my experience. One casino employee, an elderly Oriental gentleman, dealt very slowly and cautiously. After a while we made contact and established a close rapport.

Having played a lot of blackjack himself, he knew I was counting, but couldn't care less. He would count right along with me. When the deck was fat, he would deal down to the very last card, but when it soured, he immediately shuffled. The net effect was that I was playing against choice decks ninety percent of the time. I have averaged $1,000 an hour playing against this delightful old man. With playing conditions like this, it is hard to lose.

A Partnership—Not a Contest

When I win, I try to make the dealer feel as though he participated—as if he has contributed to a worthy charity. I never rejoice over having "beaten" him, but feel, rather, that the two of us have teamed up in a joint effort. This way he feels that he too has won. If I lose, I accept full responsibility for the setback. I'll say something like, "It's not your fault, baby, I blew it. You did everything you could to help, but they [the cards] weren't falling right. I want you to know, just the same, that I'm thankful for your help and we'll try again soon." With this I'll make a final bet for him, despite the loss. Often the dealer will protest, "Hey, you don't have to do that after the way I treated you today." "Bullshit," I say. "You treated me fine and you deserve a hell of a lot more; come on, deal one last hand so we can book you a winner; then at least one of us will have a little something to show for today." Giving me many thanks he says, "Come back tomorrow, you hear, and ask for me. I'll make up for this, you'll see."

Taking the "Heat" Off the Dealer

Part of the unspoken contract with the dealer is to protect him from getting into trouble for helping. Having good relationships with the floor men helps, but sometimes special situations arise, requiring support beyond the call of duty. One example of this is not taking advantage of dealer errors. Nothing will bring the sword to the dealer's neck faster than a mistake when big money is involved, and he needs a sturdy shield to stave off the incensed floor man. It costs a little, but this is an exceptional opportunity to make points with both dealer and pit boss. Take the burden off both their shoulders with conduct unheard of in gambling circles: by admitting guilt and accepting responsibility for the mishap. Once I had a $400 bet out in the midst of a luscious deck. The dealer had been going all out to help me win. He turned up a 10 and dealt me 16. I turned the cards up and softly said, "I surrender." In the midst of the noisy casino he didn't hear me, turned up a 3, and broke. A pit boss was watching, rushed over to the table, and snapped, "What's going on here?" Before the dealer could respond, I said that I had wanted to surrender but had not spoken loudly enough—"Take half my bet, it's my fault." The pit boss's scowl melted, and he said, "That's very gentlemanly of you, and we would do the same for you." Then he left. The dealer, his heart still thumping in his chest, said quietly, "Thanks, buddy. You saved my ass that time." Our partnership burgeoning, he began to furnish me with keys to the casino coffers.

On another occasion I had $500 bet and caught a 12. The dealer showed a 10. Naturally, the deck was rich. I showed him my hand and hesitated. "You're okay," he whispered. I stuck my cards under my chips, and he busted. A pit boss came over and idly inquired why I had stood on 12. "You musta known something," he quipped. "Nah," I said, "I've tried everything else and lost, so I decided before he even dealt that I was going to stand if he dealt me a 'stiff' (12–16)." The floor man laughed and ambled away. "Pretty quick thinking," the dealer said, smiling. "You're all right with me." I made a bet for him and replied, "You're my man," and we went happily along, our secret closely guarded.

Fighting Poison with Kindness

Beneficent dealers are by no means universal. Some dealers view the money as their own or let their egos get in the way; some take their pent-up anger out on the public, blaming them for their boredom. Whatever the source, some dealers are openly hostile, especially to counters. They feel that a counter is taking unfair advantage, and think they need to be on their toes catching all his moves to prevent a loss. There are two ways to handle this situation. The first is to leave at once and find a more cordial dealer. The second is to try to draw him out of his shell and recruit him as part of your team. I prefer the second approach, if the resistance is not too formidable. Draw him into conversation, ask advice, make liberal bets for him—anything you think will reach him. If all else fails, resort to "I" language. For example, "*I* really feel bad when you won't talk to me. I don't mind losing, but I care about having fun and enjoying it. Go ahead and beat me, but grant me the small favor of an occasional word. You seem like a nice enough guy. What's eating you?" If after several attempts, he still doesn't respond, don't fight it. Thank him quietly and move on.

The one thing that must be avoided is striking back out of anger. I have seen counters make horrendous scenes when a dealer shuffled up every time the deck got good. I think it's better not to show the slightest reaction, as if I couldn't care less when he shuffled. If he wants to outsmart me, I let him. Sometimes this apparent nonchalance is enough to change the dealer's outlook. If his subversive antics seem to have no effect, he may back off on his own. If I become belligerent, I'm likely to expose myself and wind up in the desert sun.

Dealers Who Count

About one out of seven dealers can recognize a counter. One in a hundred can actually count. They may suspect you of counting whenever they see wide fluctuations in bet size. If someone bets $5 on the first two hands, then $100 on the third, most dealers will shuffle up, more as a reflex action than anything else. They are trained to break the deck when players make widely divergent bets. For this reason it is important to make your bet increases appear natural. I never increase my bet unless I have won the previous hand and can idly "let the bet ride." To do this I ignore the fact that I have just been paid and leave all the chips out on the next hand. Remember, this type of behavior is common for high rollers, so it attracts little or no attention. But if you have been betting $100 on each hand and a bunch of little cards comes out and you jack your bet up to $500, you virtually guarantee a shuffle. You may as well wear a big red "C" on your chest to let the house know you are counting.

When the dealer is counting along with you, this compounds the difficulty of your task. How can you throw a bloodhound like this off your scent? The same tricks work—be humble and inflate his ego. Most counting dealers will let you know how good they are. They will tell you their exploits and attempt to convince you of their competence. Go quietly! Revere their brilliance! I will frequently ask their advice on the play of difficult situations and, when their council works out, thank them liberally, acknowledging their wisdom. I ask them if we couldn't switch places—I deal and they play. I'll offer to let them play my money so they can book me a winner. In short, I give them the credit they are seeking, and they reciprocate by protecting my secret and helping me as much as possible. Instead of pitting myself against them, challenging them to prove who is the better counter, I surrender immediately, turning up my neck in defeat and begging for mercy. Taking pity on me, *they* take responsibility for my play. Now their ego is at stake to see that I win rather than lose. They have been transposed from dealer to player. It is their money and pride being wagered. Now they will go to the whip to see that I win. My money has become theirs, and I go all out to pump up their ego, garnering a bit more treasure in the process.

Dealer Feedback to Pit Bosses

Anyone who wins in Las Vegas is suspect, because this is an uncommon event. Granted, it could be a fluke, but when it happens fairly regularly, it raises some eyebrows. The duty of explaining a win falls on the floor

man. After ruling out cheating, he tries to ascertain if
the dealer and player are in cahoots. This possibility
excluded, he asks the dealer for an evaluation of the
player. Is he counting or is he just lucky? Here the
dealer can be most helpful, if he chooses. If he says you
play foolishly, are just lucky and having a good time, it
can keep the pit boss off your back for some time. However, if he says you're counting and should be carefully
watched, the forces of evil will close in on you like a
swarm of satanic priests.

If the dealer likes you, and you are a significant con-
tributor of "goodies," he will play dumb and keep the
heat off you. But if you threaten him, he will bring the
pit bosses to you like a blanket of smog, choking off
your play. So remember, *never* antagonize anyone.
Make no enemies and be nicest to those you like least.
Negative feelings and vendettas are impediments to the
plunder you seek. Harness them.

A Gift, Not a Tip

When a new dealer begins, I will make a small bet
for him on the very first hand, saying, "Okay, partner,
I just want to show you where my heart is. I'm on your
team. Let's make a bundle together." This immediately
establishes the partnership concept. To lighten the atmosphere, I may say, "Now look, play this like it was
your own," implying that he has some control over the
play of the hand.

In a recent court ruling, dealers won a major victory.
The court ruled that all monies given to dealers are
gifts—not tips—and as such are not taxable. The logic
is that tips are given for services (as to a waitress or
hairdresser), but no one tips a dealer *because* he is

dealing. Instead, after winning, they give him a reward in gratitude. The court ruled that technically this is a gift. Knowledge of this ruling can rapidly endear you to a dealer. When I make that first bet for him I say, "This is a gift, not a tip, and I want you to treat it as such in all ways." Often I will call over a pit boss as witness, "If anyone should inquire, this bet is a gift I am wagering for the dealer, right?" Smiles all around. I have found this bit of puff very helpful for making initial contact.

The other times I like to bet for dealers are near the end of choice decks, when they have the option to deal or shuffle. Often a bet will "tip" him in favor of dealing one last hand. This accomplishes a dual purpose. First, he has dealt a hand in which you have a high probability of success; second, he is likely to win his bet. The more he makes, the happier he is. He becomes conditioned to dealing in these marginal situations.

In particularly good decks, I will let the dealer's bet ride. Let's say I have bet $5 for the dealer, and we win. He now has $10. Rather than give it to him, I bet it for him on the next hand (the deck warranting, of course). If we win again, he now has a $20 gift—not bad for a few minutes of work—and it has only cost me $5! The dealer cannot fail to notice that he wins a majority of the time when I bet for him. This further solidifies the partnership idea, drawing him farther from the role of dealer to that of the player. I never bet for the dealer in lean decks. It accomplishes no useful purpose, and we are likely to lose anyway.

Don't Bite the Hand That Feeds You

Some counters go out of their way to injure and insult dealers. They view them as the enemy and want to "rub it in" when they win. One man pulled the most unbelievable stunt I've ever seen. He was counting, and the dealer was accommodating, dealing far down into the deck. The player won steadily. After an hour he had amassed $2,500 in profits. To be exact, he had $2,550 —twenty-five $100 chips and two $25 chips. He had not made a single bet for the dealer. He started to leave and the dealer said facetiously, "You got enough? Thanks for the bets." The counter paused. "I'm sorry," he said, seeming genuine. "Here, I'll bet this $50 for you." The dealer smiled and dealt. The man got a blackjack and the dealer paid him $75. He now had $125. "Let it ride," the man said. As if the cards were taking justice into their own hands, the player got another blackjack. "Let it ride," he barked. Now $312.50 was at stake. The dealer blanched a little and dealt. The player was dealt a 19 and the dealer showed a 6. The player showed his hand to the dealer, who elatedly started to reach for his hole card. "Wait a second," snapped the player, "hit me!" In his astonishment the dealer was immobilized. "What did you say?" he pleaded. "You heard me," the player answered roughly. "Hit me!" The dealer's face became taut with anger. Reluctantly he turned the top card—an 8. The player shrugged, looking the dealer straight in the eye—"Well, you can't say I didn't bet for you, chum." He walked away laughing. Is it any wonder dealers hate counters?

Ambitious Dealers

Dealers grow up to be pit bosses. Nearly all the floor men are selected from the ranks of dealers, and competition is sometimes cutthroat. Some dealers will try to "finger" counters, to add an extra feather to their headdress. By continually "proving" themselves, they think they will be chosen when promotion time comes around. Most often they frustrate their purpose, because the current pit bosses feel threatened and dislike being "one-upped" by an ambitious subordinate. Unaware that these actions may be detrimental to their cause, some dealers will persist in their attempt to look smart, and may cause trouble for the unsuspecting counter. One of these types approached a friend of mine who is an excellent twenty-one player, asking if he knew me, looking for verification of his suspicions. My friend claimed he had never seen me before, and said that even if he had, "I'm not being paid to rat." Ignoring the hint, the dealer continued to try to get a line on me. Tipped off by my buddy, I avoided this dealer, but he would crane his neck from adjacent tables and try to get a reading from dealer friends of mine. I discovered he had pumped them for information during breaks. Finally, although on shaky grounds, he broached a pit boss with his opinion. The floor man happened to be a close acquaintance of mine and promptly told the dealer, "Listen, your job is to deal the cards, add them up right, and make the correct payoffs—nothing more —got it?" "I was just trying to protect the joint," the dealer argued. "Just protect yourself, and don't get out of line."

Now it was important for me to smooth the dealer's ruffled feathers. There's no telling who he knows, or how he got his coveted job, and I didn't want him to go above the pit boss and cause a conflict. I began chatting and going to coffee with him. Slowly he warmed. At last he confronted me: "Do you count when you play?" "I can usually add to twenty-one," I replied in jest. "Come on, level with me, are you using Thorp or Revere?" I said, "All I do is watch the aces. When there are a lot of aces left, I increase my bet; when the aces are out, I cut back." Pacified, he said, "That won't get the money." "Who's interested in money? I just like having a good time." "Well, I'm sure glad you're not counting," he said. "You know, I thought you were." I shrugged and changed the subject. The next day, my dealer friends reported that this fellow's attitude had totally changed. He had spread the word that I was "no threat," and told everyone what a nice guy I was. He had discovered my "secret" of counting aces and felt like Sherlock Holmes uncovering a set of well-hidden fingerprints. Ego salved, he no longer hassled me.

Some Helpful Hints

When playing for important money, you can take liberties not generally afforded the smaller player. Frequently you will be given the dealer of your choice. Naturally you should select those who are most cordial and furnish the best playing conditions—dealing out most of the cards. Most helpful, I have found, are those dealers who want me to win. Sometimes when the game is not being closely watched, our "partnership" has gotten away with larceny. On one occasion I had five cards totaling 17. The dealer had a 10 up and a 7 in the hole —also a 17. Unwittingly, he collected my bet of $400. When I pointed out his error, calling attention to the tie hand, he quickly reimbursed me with $600. Without question, I assumed the extra $200 was penance for his mistake—his way of saying "I'm sorry." Rather than risk offending him, I accepted the gesture, promptly betting for him, to let him know everything was okay.

If you play long enough, you will experience both underpayment and overpayment. Of course, you should be alert to any underpayment, gently calling attention to the error. Overpayment, on the other hand, may be handled less attentively. It is permissible to let down in these instances and allow the transaction to go unnoticed. Expressionless, add the chips to your stack and press on to the next hand without acknowledging the mistake. Some dealers I have encountered seem to have a preponderance of payment problems, usually dishing out too much. Instead of questioning their awareness, or unawareness, I accept this as a partnership contribution and reward the behavior. I never question their intentions, and they don't seem to notice the multiple errors. Everything is kept on a subliminal level, although I am convinced their helpful errors are purposeful, as they seem to disappear under pit-boss scrutiny.

Another little trick is to let the dealer see your hand, especially when he has looked at his hole card. Now, in the interest of the partnership, he can subtly assist your play. One dealer with borderline I.Q. took a real shine to me. When I showed him my hand and he knew he had me beaten, he would noticeably frown. When he had a bad card in the hole, he would beam, in anticipation of breaking. He was clearly wounded whenever he hit a stiff and made a hand. Needless to say, this type of relationship should be fostered whenever possible.

Motivated dealers can give you other significant gifts. Showing you the burn card is one such present. About half the time you can catch a glimpse of the buried card on your own, but with a little cooperation, you can increase this to over seventy-five percent. I like to broach this subject gingerly, even with responsive dealers: "You know, you are the fastest 'burner' I've ever seen. I never see the card you burn." "That's nothing," he retorts, "I can bury a lot faster." "Yeah, let's see," I say laughingly. He responds with a lightning-fast burn, the card whipping around and under the deck almost invisibly. "That's unbelievably fast," I acknowledge. "Now, let's see how *slow* you can burn." A knowing smile crosses his lips, and he starts burying, clumsy as a drunk.

Seeing the burn card is a big advantage. Combine this with the bottom card and you pick up .2–.3 percent. Over a year's play, this figure can become staggering. Some dealers hold the deck up high when burning, making the bottom card plainly visible. In other instances, I pull a little caper that allows me to see the bottom card every time. When I cut the cards, instead of keeping the deck parallel, I tilt it slightly, raising the side nearest me and thus exposing the bottom card. With a little practice this can be accomplished imperceptibly. Combined with dealer help on the burn, this provides the desired extra edge.

Female vs. Male Dealers

A complete description of female interaction with female dealers can be found in the chapter on "Women." Here it is only pertinent to point out some fundamental differences in approaching the two sexes. Male interaction with male dealers revolves around establishing a feeling of camaraderie and humor, to establish a joint effort and convert them from the role of dealer to player. In male interaction with women dealers, sexual overtones creep in. The relationship tends to become mutually flirtatious, and in the process the female dealer tends to facilitate your play. Avoid consummating these relationships; leave them at the table, to be taken up in your next twenty-one encounter. The more intimate your conversation, the greater the likelihood of success and the more bountiful her help.

With older women I have found a mildly flirtatious conviviality most effective. Here, recognition and regard go a long way and may find an especially receptive home, as these women are frequently ignored. Passed over for the favors of their younger peers, these women often become resentful and hostile. However, this hostility quickly evaporates when exposed to a little T.L.C. Again, if you make them feel important, they will generally reciprocate.

Tells

A tell is inadvertent information given by a dealer about his hand. It may be a mannerism or other idiosyncrasy that "tells" his hand, giving the player a reading on the dealer's hole card. Human beings are creatures of habit, and when confronted with a repetitive activity, like dealing twenty-one all day, habits are likely to develop. To the observant player, these signs are just as clear as reading street signs. An unsuspecting dealer may broadcast his hand as surely as he would by letting you peek at his hole card.

Tells are most prevalent when the dealer shows a 10. Now he must look at his bottom card to see if he has blackjack. He then knows his hand and is vulnerable to "telling." When the dealer has a 4 in the hole, it may look at first glance like an ace, so he often does a double take. Whenever you see a dealer look twice at his hole card, suspect a 4. Another situation in which tells are common is when the dealer finds a 10 in the hole, giving him a formidable pat hand. His reaction to this powerful hand often forms a predictable pattern. He may look away, feigning nonchalance, knowing he has a winner, or he may smooth the border of the cards, making sure the top and bottom card are neatly arranged, tidying his "duke." Some dealers will point to your hand when they have a strong hand. This will have the effect of hurrying you. Since they are not drawing, they point to your hand to hurry the play along. However, when they must draw, having a bad card in the hole, they will no longer point, merely hesitate in anticipation of your decision. There is no reason to hurry you if they have to draw, because their hand is not pat. Other dealers will do the exact opposite, pointing to your hand when they have a bad card in the hole (a "stiff"), and not pointing when they have a pat hand. Unconsciously, they would like you to draw and break before they have a chance to bust themselves.

When a dealer knows his hole card, watching his eyes can be very revealing. Some dealers will look down when they have a good hand, while firmly meeting your stare when they are "stiff." Others, the reverse. Some smile when they are "there," others grimace. One dealer really had a corker of a tell. Every time he looked at a 10 in the hole, he would draw air through his two front teeth, making a slurping sound like sucking up the last of a malted. This was so obvious I was embarrassed, feeling sure a pit boss would notice. None did, and I appeared to make many exceptional decisions when actually I was being "told" how to play my cards. In one instance I actually hit a hard 18, drawing a 3 to beat a 20. But the dealer had slurped, and I was certain that my 18 was worthless.

I have had dealers stop dead in the middle of a conversation when they have a big hand. This momentary pause affords the opportunity to either surrender or hit in circumstances when I would normally stand, even though the odds may be six to one against, when drawing. I am a near cinch to lose if I stand.

To pick up a tell, watch all the dealer's reactions and movements without drawing conclusions. Observe how long he looks at his hole card and how he arranges it. Notice the position of his hands and body. Study the way he holds the cards, his facial expression, and his attitude. After a while, a pattern of behavior will emerge. When you suspect a tell, confirm it by predicting to yourself what the dealer's card is likely to be over the next few hands based on the tip-off you have observed. If you are correct, act on this knowledge. Continue to take advantage of the situation as long as the behavior persists. One dealer would take a long look at his hole card when he saw a face card. When he peeked at a small card, he would quickly release it, encouraging me to act on my hand. After a few days he seemed to notice his tip-off. After making a few blunders, I realized he had reversed his behavior, now taking long looks at small cards and fast looks at 10's. I changed my play accordingly. A few weeks later this dealer disappeared. I was told he had "quit."

I find that I pick up a great deal of information if I show the dealer my hand. Now he knows his hand and mine; there is no question of where things stand. He knows if he has me beat or not. Sometimes I will ask innocently, "Do you have twenty again?" The intonation of his response can be very revealing. Once I had a $500 bet and was dealt an ace/7. The dealer showed a 10 and looked at her hole card. As I showed her my hand, I whispered, "Have a twenty?" "No," she said, her voice rising at the end of the word. I interpreted this to mean she had 19. I hit the hand and caught an 8. I now had 16. Normally I would stand on 16 against a 10, when the deck is rich with 10's, hoping that the dealer has a small card and will break. But in this instance I strongly suspected that the dealer had a pat 19. I drew again—a 4, giving me 20. As she had intimated, she flipped over a 9. Our brief interaction made a $1,000 difference. Instead of losing $500 on the hand, I won $500. She had responded to my question without thinking. She thought that by saying "No" to my question about having a 20, I would stand on my ace/7 (soft 18), and she would win with 19. The inflection in her voice, however "told" me her exact hole card.

I learn a lot from watching the dealer's reaction to my cards, even if he is trying to deceive me. Unless he is devilishly clever, his attempts at deception will also fall into a readable pattern. Watching the pupils of his eyes can tell you if he's lying or not. When a person tells a lie, his pupils contract; if he tells the truth, his pupils tend not to change or even to dilate a bit. Also, when he is nervous about his hand, his pupils will contract; when content, they will dilate or not change. There are individual differences in the degree of pupillary response, but on the whole this is a very reliable signal. The larger the pupil, the more easily discernible its reactivity. One dealer had amazing pupillary response. When I showed him my hand and he was beaten, his pupils became pinholes. If he had the better hand, they expanded like dark pools. It was like adjusting the lens aperture on a camera. No matter how he tried to deceive me (and this particular fellow wanted to win), his eyes gave him away.

On the other hand, a certain dealer had me totally confused. His large pupils never seemed to change. It looked as though he was always happy with his hand and never lied, but I knew this couldn't be true. Several months later I found out he had been fired and was in a methadone detoxification program for heroin addiction. Drugs will throw off pupillary readings, so if you find dealers with large fixed pupils, rely on other tells.

Showing the dealer my hand can have a second positive spin-off. Let's say the dealer shows a 10, I have 12, and I show him the hand, saying, "Hit me." I now catch a 3. Often, if the dealer is stiff, he will start to reach for his cards. This is a very reliable sign—he will be stiff about ninety percent of the time. Whenever I observe him reaching or leaning toward his hand, I immediately stand. Most dealers will wait patiently when they have a face card in the hole unless intentionally trying to deceive the player.

Despite my acute interest in subtle tip-offs, I try to avoid setting up a contest with the dealer where he is trying to throw me off track and I am trying to second-guess him. I much prefer cooperative relationships. To foster cooperation, I bet for the dealer each time I win a hand I would normally lose, whether the information that enabled me to win was supplied voluntarily or involuntarily. This, combined with an open, friendly attitude, tends to cement a cordial interaction instead of creating a competitive atmosphere. It also reinforces desirable unconscious behavior.

The dealer can be a tremendous asset, so treat him kindly. Meet his needs, and he will handsomely reward you. Remember, dealers grow up to be pit bosses, so you will be in contact for many years. It pays to establish long-standing amiable relationships.

10

The Pit Boss:
Friend or Foe?

The pit boss, or floor man, supervises the blackjack games. His is the onerous task of detection—the cheaters, chip hustlers, scam artists—and the counters. He is judge and jury over any controversy. Overseeing several games simultaneously, the pit boss is on his feet for eight consecutive hours, pacing from table to table like a caged animal. Constantly alert to would-be thieves, he surveys his domain, watching bets and pay-offs, exchanging chips for money, and writing credit slips. Each time a deck is removed from play, he scrutinizes it for bent or marked cards. He counts each old deck to make sure no cards are missing or added.

Knowing that most cheating originates from the "inside," he watches the dealers for chip siphoning and intentional "dumping" to a player. Many schemes involve dealer-player partnerships, so the pit boss is especially alert to this interaction. A strange combination of banker and detective, his role demands caution and suspicion. Although public relations is an integral part of his duties, this aspect often goes wanting, suppressed by an overriding wariness that frequently dominates his conduct. His superiors are constantly on his back, demanding more income per table, and tighter controls. When an incident escapes the pit boss's watchful eye, he is called on the carpet, chewed out, and possibly fired. Years of this constant stress hardens and fatigues him. Work becomes a chore, and he may vent his frustrations on other floor men, dealers, and patrons. Making less money than the dealers since he gets no tips, he harbors deep-seated resentment. His is a thankless job with few friends. He tends to be lonely and sullen, frequently passive, then lashes out, his tolerance overwhelmed by tension marbled with monotony. Taking umbrage at every quarter—dealer, player, and superior —he shields himself by withdrawing into a protective shell, feeding on suspicion and becoming a cold, estranged "loner."

The pit boss is obviously unhappy with this situation. He doesn't want to be disliked and mistrusted, yet experience dictates caution. I have found that by slowly drawing him out, encouraging open interaction without consequence, I have been able to establish close relationships that have paid whopping dividends.

How to warm these glacier-like personalities, that is the question. First, I don't play their "game." Combating their suspicious behavior with warmth and openness, I grope for a topic of conversation, a thread of interest that can be developed and expanded upon, forming the roots of a relationship. I lighten the atmosphere with playful good humor. Remember, it's all just a game! As with the dealer, I make contact, making the pit boss feel welcome in my presence. I truly value his friendship and advice, and communicate my appreciation. As our relationship grows, he feels wanted and respected.

Like the dealer, he must be made to feel part of the team, rather than an isolated authority figure, ready to intervene at any moment. I try to communicate respect for his knowledge, accumulated over the years, not disdain for his attitude and power. Instead of withdrawing when he approaches, I show him my cards and ask advice. When given, I tend to accept his counsel. If the decision turns out to be correct, his ego is inflated, as I acknowledge his sagacity; if incorrect, he feels obligated, since the mistake was *his* doing, and he has an image to protect.

When the pit boss loosens up, I further involve him in the net. I offer to have him "squeeze out" a hand for me for luck or, better still, to have him play a hand or two for me. That's right! He plays and I watch. This costs very little, as most floor men are basically competent players. Some get so wrapped up in this little charade that they refuse to show me the hand until the play is finished—it's *their* hand, not mine! This suits me perfectly. We now have formed a working unit—the pit boss, the dealer, and me—with one unified goal in mind, winning! Instead of the pit boss feeling that some counter is trying to cheat him out of his money, he has fun contributing to your winnings. His ego needs, normally served by uprooting undesirables, are now filled by a sense of participation and contribution that I recognize and appreciate. When I'm running bad, I will call over one of my pit boss friends "for luck." Or, prior to sitting down to play, I will have a chat with him, asking which tables are his, because I *want* to play in his section. Instead of avoidance, I seek contact and involvement. Usually pit bosses are eager to reciprocate. I try to be as natural and cordial as possible at the blackjack table in an attempt to lower the tension level.

I treat the money with casual neglect and, after a while, the pit bosses drop their guard despite the high stakes. Their typically skittish behavior is misplaced and inappropriate here, and they do their best to go along with this unusual and pleasant situation.

I readily concede that they have the superior skills and that I fully expect to be beaten. If, by some miracle, I win, I give them full credit for the "windfall," emphasizing the fortuity of having such competent help. I have received inordinate amounts of help from pit bosses, some undergoing complete reversals of their behavior. One day I was playing at a favorite watering hole, and a strange floor man was watching me play. Quietly I asked the dealer who he was. He informed me that he was new—this was only his second day. The pit boss observed me from a distance, and I could tell he had a thorough knowledge of the game (after a while you can "sense" these things). I abbreviated my play and cashed in my chips. On the way out I stopped and introduced myself to this new face. He was affable and seemed grateful for the diversion. He told me he had once been in casino management and had himself been a player, years ago. He said I played well, and although he had only watched me for ten minutes, "noticed no leaks in my play." Downplaying this aspect, I told him I tried hard, but to no avail, having lost fortunes at the game over the years. Genuinely concerned, he confided that the game could be beaten, and gave me the names of Thorp's and Revere's books. On my next visit he asked if I had read them. I told him I had been unable to find them at my local bookstore. Next day, when I returned, a package awaited me in a plain brown wrapper. Inside was a copy of *Beat the Dealer*.

On my next trip he again inquired if I had read the

book. I said that I had, but that it was too complicated, filled as it was with ratios, formulas, and all. I said I would rather remain ignorant and enjoy the game. Besides, if I needed advice, I would rather get it from him instead of some mathematics professor. After all, he had spent years at blackjack, both inside and out, and knew the game thoroughly; I didn't need anyone else. He readily obliged. I became his protégé. He would chide me when he thought I made an error and encourage me when he agreed with a decision. I must come clean, however. I did have a slight edge: in close decisions, for example with 12 when the dealer showed a 2, my "mentor" would look at the dealer's hole card *before* coming up with a definitive recommendation. As you can well imagine, this made for a certain degree of accuracy when he assisted. He was elated when I won, especially when I emphasized its rarity before he started coaching me. For hours he would camp at my left elbow and we would consult on virtually every hand. I let him control the betting pace as well as make the final decision on the play of the hand. He played very well, so we had few differences in any case, although I purposefully created a few for effect. With the count at plus 6 and one-third of the deck left, he insisted I split 10's with the dealer showing a 5. Vociferously I protested: "I was told *never* to split 10's." "Trust me!" he said. "You know best, Peter," I said. I split the 10's and was dealt a 10 and an ace, 20 and 21 respectively. I won both hands. The dealer sharted to shuffle, but Peter stopped him. "You've got enough for one more," he barked. "Let your bet ride," he said to me. Again I protested: "That's a thousand dollars I have riding." "We've got the best of it," he said. "Believe me!" "Whatever you say—you're the boss." I won the next hand by a whisker—my 20 versus the dealer's 19. I breathed a sigh of relief, trying to appear shaken. Peter gave me a triumphant wink and strutted away, well pleased with his handiwork.

No less than seven pit bosses have given me twenty-one lessons. I have been given two copies of Revere's book, and one copy of Thorp's. In addition, I have had numerous tutorials on how to play one or another count system. In each instance I listen dutifully, asking appropriate questions and demonstrating some skepticism. Resolved that I will try *their* system, I once again plunge into the breach. Now if I win, they are pleased. It also makes it very difficult to bar me when I am only doing what they taught me. Naturally, I credit them for making a dramatic difference in my play.

Many pit bosses will spontaneously bring up the subject of counting. Some try to test me: "You counting, Ian?" I have found an exaggeration to be the best response to this question. I'll say, "I don't count, I memorize every card." This usually gets a chuckle, or at least a snort, out of them. Another floor man approached me and said, "You play pretty well." I said I had been playing for years, and I had learned the secret of playing twenty-one—watch the aces and bet more when the aces are in the deck. I combine this with good money management, doubling up when I win the preceding hand if the aces are right. A group of bosses watched me play several sessions, and I overheard their conversation: "Look, he doubled up and all the aces are gone. The count is plus 5, he must be counting." Another pit boss countered, "Nah, he won the last hand, so he's doubling up." Obligingly, I cut back after losing the ensuing hand. "See," the floor man said, "the deck's still gangbusters and he cut back. He can't play at all.

There's nothing to worry about." They disbanded. I won *over* $5,000 in four sessions "counting aces."

Gambling books have become popular, and many people have heard of terms like "counting" and money management, although they don't really understand them. Rather than shun these words, I use them improperly. The impression this creates is that I know just enough to lose, and I support that notion.

I give the impression that I don't think twenty-one can be beaten. I am constantly reiterating how much I have lost since I started playing. This makes each win seem small by comparison. For further reinforcement I'll say something like, "I'd like to have the money I've lost at this game. If you'd just give me back what I've lost, I'd never play again." During the course of our conversation, the pit boss may tell me about counters. I say that sounds like a lot of work and would take all the fun out of the game. One pit boss told me that "Thorp counters can't play, so don't learn that or we won't be able to have fun together any more. We have to keep one step ahead of the players, you know." I told him I had no intention of learning Thorp's or anyone else's system. He seemed relieved. Over the next four days, I won $16,000 on his shift without arousing suspicion.

Although all pit bosses are aware that counters exist, few floor men can count accurately. But many have a sixth sense for counters. Somehow they pick up on the vibes and link them with changes in bet size. Like an ant identifying an edible morsel, their antennae wave tentatively, sensitive to an indefinable difference in feeling between the counter and the regular player. Still, most can't be sure, but if they suspect, they may institute countermeasures just to be safe, *unless* they are motivated to either ignore, or overlook, their intuition. I go all out to help them in this oversight. I try to make their job more enjoyable by adding levity and interest. I have fun when I play, and this spirit can be infectious to even the well-inoculated floor men. Often they find themselves caught up in the excitement of squeezing out cards or doubling down for high stakes, especially when they have been drawn into an active role as counselor or, better still, as player.

I view the pit boss as a business client. After all, playing blackjack is an exceptionally lucrative business, and the good graces of the floor man facilitates results, so he must be courted. In addition to intangible rewards like respect, recognition, and friendship, I frequently furnish floor men with small tokens of my appreciation. Once, while in Hawaii, I picked up an entire shipment of silk shirts of every size and description. Spending a good deal of effort carefully sizing up my pit boss client's taste, I select a shirt or two that is "just him." A little elegant gift wrapping and my offering is ready.

How it is presented is nearly as important, if not more so, than the gift itself. The presentation is surrounded with warmth and appreciation, underlining the fact that its recipient is a special person, deserving of lavish attention. Las Vegas thrives on money, influence (popularly called "juice"), status, and favors, so gifts are most appropriate. But beware! Gifts must be in line with what the people in contact with you perceive as fair. I have made some atrocious blunders in this regard. In one club I had doled out about ten shirts, two to each shift boss, and one to each assistant boss. Unwittingly I had overlooked one assistant. He had been particularly cordial to me, providing me with excellent playing conditions and no heat. One day he came over to me and said straight out: "Pal, what do I have to do to earn a shirt?" I felt a stab of contrition. I selected one of my finest, and presented it to him on my next trip, duly apologetic. Fortunately, he was appeased. I could have blown my entire set-up if, in his resentment, he had decided to cause trouble rather than confront me. As a rule I distribute presents by position, not by emotion. Which pit bosses you like is inconsequential. I cater to the casino power structure, paying tribute to the decision makers. The head pit boss, or shift boss, makes the ultimate decision on who stays and plays and who is barred, so he is a prime candidate for wooing, regardless of his personality.

One of these types may well be the most obnoxious person I've ever met. Short, fat, bald, and cigar-smoking, he is universally disliked by subordinates and customers as well. Never having a kind word for anyone, he stomps up and down the pit, pissing and moaning at everything and everyone. His face seems frozen in a permanent scowl. It took courage to offer this troll-like being a silk shirt; it seemed like offering a Cadillac to a gorilla. Roughly he tore open the fine gift wrapping and pulled out the silken doublet. "You didn't have to do that," he growled. "I know, but I wanted to," I lied. "Well, thanks," he said curtly, and walked away. Next afternoon he was sporting his new finery, looking like a peacock who had been run over by a lawnmower. He called me over and asked if he could do anything. When I declined, he asked if I was going to play, telling me he had specially prepared a private table for me. Overwhelmed, I yielded to his entreaty. For the first time in history he seemed glad to see a player win. The dealers were thunderstruck at this new attitude and asked "What did you do to him? He looks like a con who just had his first woman in ten years." In a way, that's exactly what he'd had! It was the first attention old sourpuss had received in perhaps twenty years— and it paid off! At the time of this writing, I can still play unmolested on his shift, and invariably he dons his shirt in dress parade when I visit.

Besides giving gifts, I spend time socially with casino personnel. Lunches and dinners are common. I also try to take them to shows, major sporting events, and exhibitions. Tennis, golf, and swimming are interests shared by most bosses, and I arrange to join them in these diversions. I attempt to steer the conversation away from gambling during these social interludes, but I answer direct questions. My sob story is always the same, but I reassure them that I can afford the losses, so they needn't be concerned. Graciously I accept any advice they may extend, thanking them for their interest. Our relationship gradually becomes complementary— each fulfilling certain needs for mutual sustenance. As long as this symbiosis persists, my status as a player remains unthreatened.

This is a most atypical situation. A delicate balance exists, and it becomes unclear as to who is courting whom. Normally, the pit boss provides all the amenities for the big player. In this instance, however, benefits run both ways and the bosses appreciate the change. But I mustn't get too close. Floor men live in mortal fear of their superiors, and if word leaks out that we are close friends, collusion may be suspected. The paranoia index runs high at all echelons of casino management, so it is best not to feed it. There is a fine line that must be gingerly trod. Quiet associations out of range of watchful eyes and perked ears are best.

Pit bosses have widely divergent personalities and each yields to different handling. I find the extroverted, fast-talking, quick-witted type easiest to deal with. It is simple to set up a dialogue that directs his attention away from the twenty-one game and on to a good-natured verbal duel. These little word games become harmless fun and can sometimes be used advantageously. At one smaller casino, a vice president came to observe my play. He'd been in the business for years and knew the ropes pretty well. He was a natural con man, but was a little rusty on sophisticated twenty-one play. Gray, with black horn-rimmed glasses and a quick tongue, he constantly harangued me with verbiage, offering me this "deal" and that. The game became a bargaining contest. Sometimes he would let me surrender after I had already drawn a card, as when I had 14 against a point; on other occasions he would let me surrender various fractions of my bet, like three-eighths or one-fourth. Of course he would try to trick me into unreasonable deals. Once he said, "I'll let you surrender one-fourth of your bet without looking." I had a very small bet out, so I agreed, feigning ignorance. He laughed heartily: "I'll tell you what," he said, "you can give me one-fourth of your chips and not play another hand." "Nah," I said, "you'd be cheating yourself out of three-fourths of my chips." He chortled and kept offering me deals. I had a big bet riding and quickly looked at my cards, a 9 and a 7—16. The dealer showed a 10. The boss had been temporarily distracted and had not seen me peek at my cards. "Can I look at one card and give up one-fourth of my bet?" I asked. "No, if you look at a card you have to give up three-eighths," he replied. "What if I don't look?" I asked. "Then one quarter is okay," he said. "How about one-eighth? You already tricked me once with that one-fourth. With one-eighth I can preserve my money a little longer," I said, probing. He laughed and said, "You want to give up one-eighth without looking—okay." The dealer took a small portion of my bet and turned up my 16. "Whew," I sighed, "that was a good decision for a change." I had saved several hundred dollars with this little caper, and it had cost me less than $25 to set it up—a pretty fair return on an investment.

Now the old man was really getting into the swing of things, making deals right and left. I was playing at a private table and a large crowd had gathered, enjoying the bartering more than anything. The deck ripened, and I placed two $500 bets, the house limit. The dealer turned a 6. I looked at my first hand, a 12. I hesitated. "What's wrong?" the old boy quipped. "Got a problem?" I showed him my hand and said, "I'm just trying to decide whether to hit this or not." "Would it help if I showed you the dealer's hole card?" he asked. "It sure couldn't hurt," I replied. With that, he flipped over the dealer's hole card—a 10. "You probably want to surrender now," he teased, "he's got your 12 beat by 4." "I probably should," I said, "but I think I'll just stand." On to the next hand—20. "Can I split these 10's?" I asked. "Sure," he said, "if you've got the balls." "I did the last time I checked," I said with a downward glance, and split the two face cards. I got a 3 on the first and another 10 on the second. "Can I split again?" I requested. "As many times as you like, baby," he urged. Finally I was playing five hands at $500 each. My totals were 12, 13, 17, 18, and 19. When I had no more 10's to split, the dealer finally drew—the case 5, for 21. As he collected my bets I said, "That's the only way you could have squeezed $2,500 out of me. Now I'm really hot. How about raising the limit?" I whipped out a $10,000 bundle, and he accommodated by raising the

limit to $1,000. I varied my bets from $200 to $1,000.
The chips went back and forth while the dialogue continued at a furious pace. Then the deck got very juicy.
I bet $1,000 and once again the dealer turned a 6. I
had 20 and said, "How about that hole card crap
again?" "It'll cost ya' this time," he replied. "It cost me
plenty last time," I retorted weakly. "Give me $200 and
I'll show you," he offered. Not one to refuse a bargain,
I agreed. Again the dealer flipped over a 10 to give him
sixteen. Flashes of repeat performance swept through
my mind but I suppressed the negative thoughts. I split
the 10's and was promptly dealt two more 10's; I split
both hands again. Now I had four hands at $1,000 each.
He dealt—a 4 to the first 10, a 6 to the next, then two
more 10's. Again I split, I was running out of room.
A hum permeated the growing gallery. Six hands at
$1,000 each. Now he dealt an ace, a 9, a 5 (fortunately
the last one) and an 8. My totals were 14, 16, 21, 19,
15, and 18 respectively. The dealer hit himself with a
7—a bust! I had won $6,000 in a single hand (less the
$200 I had to pay to see the hole card), and I decided
not to press my luck any further, calling it a night. I
went for coffee with the executive, and we had a good
laugh over our experience. I wish I could get something
like that "on" *every* time I play.

Most floor men are more subdued (and have less
authority) than this wily old codger. Gentlemanly, quiet
conversation mixed with an occasional humorous antic
to lighten things up are in order with this kind of person. Tasteful clowning seems to be generally appreciated by all. I may turn a somersault in the middle of
the casino to change my luck, or spread my chips all
over the table on some outrageous pretense. Again
their attention is misdirected. There's no telling what

I'm likely to do next, and I try to keep drumming up amusements for the court.

My finest hour came at a small downtown Las Vegas casino. I was in a rare mood and felt playful. One of those fast-talking types was supervising my game and we hit it off immediately. I started betting small, but before long had them drag the $100 chips out of moth balls. I won steadily, if not dramatically, and was about $2,000 ahead after a couple of hours. I needed to take a break, but the pit bosses refused to let me go. They were convinced I only counted aces and doubled my bet after winning, and thought it was only a matter of time until they would break me. I got up to leave but the head pit boss took me aside and pleaded: "Stay a while longer. We like your company and really want you to play more." I said, "The only way you're going to get me to stay is if you get me a room, a shower, a hooker, and pick up the tab." Immediately he agreed. I went upstairs, took a shower, dissipated my excess tension with the lady, and returned to the gaming tables. In the next hour I won another $1,500. I got up and began collecting my chips. Again the chief appeared from nowhere and asked if I'd join him for breakfast. I was hungry and needed another break, so I agreed. During breakfast he worked me over, entreating me to play just a bit more. Being a weak soul, I finally agreed, won another $1,000, and fought my way to the exits, promising to return again soon.

I love being hustled like this by pit bosses. I'm not easy, but I can be had. At one club in northern Nevada, I'm a regular. I wait until a table empties, then sit down. The pit bosses all know me and ask, "What'll it be, Ian?" "I don't know," I say. "What limit do *you* want me to play. I'll play for fives, twenty-fives or hundreds, whatever you say." "In that case let's make it a hundred," he says resolutely. "That's okay with me, if that's what you want," I reply. If I win, I thank him for *his* idea; if I lose, I congratulate him for his competence in hustling me into a big game, and recommend to his superior that he be given a raise.

At another club, I was playing with $25 chips. On instructions from the pit boss, the dealer kept paying me with $100 chips, swapping my $25's to keep the payoffs straight. Before long my supply of $25 chips was completely exhausted. I glanced over at the knowing pit boss and asked, "What kind of a scam is this? If I didn't know better, I'd think you were trying to hustle me into playing for hundreds." "You got it, buddy," he said with a wink. "Okay," I said, "I sure hope my luck holds out." It did.

I try to meet everyone I can. I don't want to risk resentment by neglecting anyone. Working hard at remembering names and connecting them up with faces, I make notes in my diary to help my recall on future visits. I attempt to make a few key friends on each shift. Eventually someone will broach the subject of my counting at a pit-boss meeting, and I need a few friends at court to support my case and help the others see things differently.

A good example of the significance of having a few key "insiders" plead my case occurred at a large Lake Tahoe casino. I had been playing on and off for four days and had won every time I played. During my stay, I had "gotten next to" several pit bosses and a couple of shift bosses. One boss remained highly suspicious and shunned all my advances. Next day one of my newly acquired confidants told me I had caused a big stir. My name had been brought up at a meeting and all hell broke loose! The leery shift boss had convinced a few of his henchmen that I was counting and should be barred on sight. My supporter retaliated, pointing out that I had been unbelievably lucky—it was only a matter of time before the odds would catch up with me. They claimed no one could count accurately while keeping up a steady stream of chatter and constantly clowning. Besides, if there were never any winners, there wouldn't be any gambling. The recalcitrant pit boss wasn't buying. A shouting contest ensued, each tactfully implying that the other didn't know his ass from a hole in the ground. In the end my case was carried by sheer force of numbers. I carefully avoided my antagonist's shift, and continued playing in the protective custody of my fans.

11

Other Casino Games:

Someone Has to Pay for All Those Lights

With the exception of twenty-one, all casino games have fixed percentages against the player. Each roll of the dice or spin of the roulette wheel favors the house. So in the long run, if you play these games, you will lose a predictable percentage of the total dollars you wager. This percentage varies depending on the game you're playing and on which of the available betting options you select. For example, you can decrease your overall disadvantage to less than 0.5 percent by betting the "don't pass" at the crap table and laying double odds (where allowed), or you can really go up against it by playing keno, or betting the hard ways at craps, where the odds against you exceed twenty percent.

Craps is most interesting in this regard. Depending on which bets you make, the odds vary enormously, more so than in any other casino game. If you are a smart player, you can have a real run for your money with a minuscule overall disadvantage. But the unknowing (or uncaring) can get raped. The hard ways: field bet, any craps, any seven and eleven bets, should fall under the

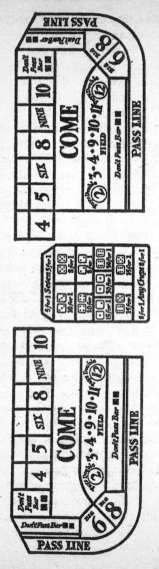

anti-usury laws, they are so extortionary. Slightly better, but still abysmal, are the number bets. The best bets are the "pass" line (betting with the shooter), and the "don't pass" line (betting against the shooter), and either taking or laying the odds. If, on the first roll, the shooter does not roll 2, 3, 7, 11, or 12, he has a "point." If he rolls this number again before rolling a 7, he wins. The odds against rolling this number before a 7 vary, depending on which number shows. Let's say the shooter rolls a 4 on his first roll. To win, he now needs a 4 before he rolls a 7. There are six combinations of dice that add up to seven: 4–3, 3–4, 5–2, 2–5, 6–1, and 1–6. Only three combinations total four: 3–1, 1–3, and 2–2. It follows that the odds of rolling a 7 prior to a 4 are 6 to 3, or 2 to 1. If you have bet the pass line and another player opens with a 4, you can back up your pass-line bet with an amount equal to your original wager. Now, if the player rolls a 4 before a 7, you win your original bet, plus *twice* your backup bet. The house pays you 2 to 1 and the odds against a 4 showing before a 7 are 2 to 1—an even-money proposition. For don't-pass players the converse obtains. Betting against the shooter, the hope is for a 7 before a 4 in the above example. The odds in favor of this occurring are 2 to 1, so they must *lay* 2 to 1 instead of taking 2 to 1—still an even-money proposition on this portion of their wager.

The odds bets in craps are the only even-money casino gamble. Each "point" pays different odds: 6 and 8 pay six to five, 5 and 9 pay three to two, and 4 and 10 pay two to one, all pays equal to the true odds. Some casinos will let you take, or lay, double odds, an amount equal to twice your initial bet. This serves to decrease the overall percentage against you. Betting the don't-pass line is slightly more profitable than betting the pass line. Combined with double odds, the percentage loss is very small indeed. Counting aside, this is the best gamble of any casino game!

Baccarat is also a decent gamble—about a one and a quarter percent disadvantage. It requires no decisions, which makes it easy to play. You can bet either on the player or on the bank. When you bet on the bank and win, you must pay a five percent commission or "vig." Of course, the bank wins more often than the players. Although very close, it is probably a little better to bet with the players.

In roulette, the house advantage leaps to over five percent no matter what you do. Red, black, odd, even, or number bets—it makes no difference. Just figure to lose $5 out of every $100 you bet—forget it!

The odds against you in keno, the wheel of fortune, and the slot machines are a joke. At best you can cut your disadvantage to a pathetic seventeen percent—$17 out of every $100 is lost. A bit rich for even the bluest blood!

Can any casino game be legitimately beaten? Probably not, although some scientists might take issue with this statement. For many years scientists have been examining whether the human mind, or more precisely, certain human minds, can influence the outcome of a seemingly random event, solely by "willing" a desired outcome. As early as the 1930s, Dr. J. B. Rhine of Duke University began experimenting with dice throwing. The subjects tried to "will" the outcome of the dice. Some experiments were done with a single die, others with six dice. The subject tried to make a specified number come up. To protect against imperfections in the dice, the number was periodically changed, so that each face was equally "willed up." In 50,000 trials the face willed came up significantly more often than predicted by chance. No less than half a dozen reputable scientists have repeated Rhine's work and verified the results. This effect is called psychokinesis, literally "motion-mind," or the ability to control motion by an act of will. Is it possible that some gamblers possess this formidable quality, or can all "win-streaks" be accounted for within the spectrum of random events?

We have all had the experience of "sensing" that something is about to happen—and then it happens. Or having a "feeling" of knowing the top card of a deck. But do we also have a number of sensations and feelings that don't pan out, remembering only those that do? This issue is certainly open to conjecture. I know a person who plays craps and always bets the same amount of money. He always bets the don't-pass line and lays the odds. He will *only* play at an empty table where he can continually throw the dice. He concentrates intensely on the desired outcome, then calls an exact combination as he releases the dice: "Five, two," he may shout when he wants a 7. Reliable sources say that since this player started shooting craps he has won 200 more bets than he has lost, in about 5,000 trials. This is a win rate of four percent! The odds of this happening purely by chance are astronomical!

Although somewhat skeptical, my mind remains open to the possibility that psychokinesis is a real phenomenon, and that some people can overcome a slight casino advantage and turn a handsome profit. This would seem to pose an interesting dilemma for the casino, so I asked a casino manager what he would do if a player, without cheating, consistently won at craps. His answer was prompt and curt: "I'd throw him out!" "But if you knew everything was on the square," I pressed, "wouldn't you think the odds would eventually catch up with him?" "Look," he said, "I don't care if the guy has a halo around his head and constantly recites Hail Marys, if he wins regularly he's out! It's not our business to figure out how a guy is winning. We're not in business to support winners while we figure out how they're doing it. If we don't like their action, that's it!"

So all you blossoming psychokinetic wizards, beware! The day may come when you are thrown into the same category as counters, and when that happens, you had better have your act together. I can hear the pit bosses furtively whispering now, "Do you think that's one of them kinetic guys?"

12

Poker:

Or Having Champions for Breakfast

It's every gambler's dream to sit down, a stranger in a high-stakes poker game, and clean up. Most Las Vegas casinos have traps to snare such dreamers. Poker has become a profitable casino-managed game, and even the posh joints now sport cardrooms. They charge each player by the hour, or take a "rake," a percentage of each pot (five to twenty percent). In a word—beware! The games are crawling with professionals, weaving intricate webs to snare the unsuspecting tourist. Las Vegas has become a final battleground for the hardened pro. Millions of dollars change hands yearly, and the locals scramble for their share of the take. When people and money get together all may not be "kosher," and this is certainly true of poker in Vegas. The local hustlers won't do anything to you—unless they can get away with it—and they have spent their whole lives learning the tricks of the trade.

I began playing poker in Vegas ten years ago. When I was in college, a wily pro took me under his wing and showed me the ropes. He organized a biweekly game, regularly fleecing the bright-eyed students. For a solid year I sat behind him and observed. For the next three years I lived off this game. It was a high-caliber, tight game, but I eked out enough to have a little extra scratch through college.

By the time I ventured the Vegas poker greens, I had learned my lessons well. I had mastered emotional control and money management and did not fall apart when losing. Being a natural ham, I knew how to dominate a game. Money didn't scare me, and I wasn't easily intimidated. And so I lit into the big time, looking innocent and rosy-cheeked in my college jacket (although long out of school). The locals salivated at the prospect and would doubtlessly have devoured me had I not had help. On the first night, after taking a small loss, I met a couple of budding young "Hoyles" who ran the game down to me. They had quite a "book" on all the players, and briefly described each player's style, identified partnerships,* and fingered the cheats. Armed with this barrage of information, I was able to control the game and won steadily. As it turned out, my biggest asset was the ego of the pro. Seeing a young innocuous new face, the locals tried to steamroll over me. Since I was supposed to lose, they would play inferior hands and act surprised when they came up second best. I would get called in unlikely situations, as the resident sharks tried to get a line on my play. I appeared ignorant and lucky as I fumbled with my chips. Winning steadily, I disappeared after several days, not returning for six months. Same plot. Another run-down of the games, then pick my spot, hit, and split. In this way I won consistently, eluding traps. Over the years I have continued to win,

* Players often team up and send signals to each other, stealing antes and setting traps (see chapter on Cheating).

although playing sparingly of late. Recently the games have become exceedingly tough. You need a scorecard to identify the teams and thieves that camp in those smoke-filled niches.

But for the pros, business goes on as usual. He keeps a neat record of his play. In it he notes the date, hours played and win or loss. He keeps an ongoing biography of the players—how much they win or lose, their mannerisms, style of play, and other tells. Studying his opponents, he looks for flaws or weaknesses in their game. He also logs potential pitfalls—teams, holdout artists, card markers, and other devious aficionados. His is a guarded existence, as he tries to stay one step ahead of the pack. But in the final analysis all the pros feed off the tourist. The visitor supports both the casinos and the locals. Some are high rollers who drunkenly stumble into an awaiting empty seat, but most are hometown champions. All year long they garner their stake in Minneapolis, Detroit, Cleveland, and such, preparing for their yearly migration to the big time. Taking a low-cost room, they spend night and day at the tables, slowly being chewed up until they go bust. Then home, again to start accumulating funds from their local games. Those who win in Vegas over the years can be counted on two hands, and they usually have an inside line, or are doing "business" with the locals.

One cagey old pro summed it up for me this way: "They all come and go—them local heroes. Very few make out. They get a rush of cards and get winners, and first thing you know they're ready to move here! Give up that lumber company in Oregon and settle right into this strawberry patch. At first they get called more by the pros, so they move out here, then go bust. I've seen 'em come and go by the busload. They come to town, play tight, and win for a while. But it ain't like home. Here the games go twenty-four hours. They play too much, play in bad games. They don't pick their spots like the locals. No, these hot shots got to be in action every day. They go up against tough competition, play long hours, and drink like fish. They're not mentally in charge like they are at their home table. Next thing you know, *they* are throwing the party. They ain't got enough con in 'em to make it here. And they don't know when they're bein' fucked. We got some real smoothies around here. Wear velvet rubbers when they fuck people. Yeah, real smooth. Most folks don't even know they've been had. Most guys around here'd think nothin' of puttin' a rattlesnake in your pocket and askin' you for a match. Yeah, I seen it all. Seen 'em come and go. We eat 'em for breakfast, them local champs."

I asked about the college champs: "College kids— ain't got no dough. Come in here and play real tight in those small-limit games. Most get ground out by the ante and rake. Others get run over, bluffed out of too many pots. Too mechanical—only want to play the nuts. You can't win here if you keep waitin' for A-B-C before you get involved. Nah, them kids get ground out before too long."

So who makes all the money? The biggest winners are the casinos that host the games. A good cardroom can net over a million a year. Fewer than ten players really cream it—making over $100,000 yearly. Most big-time players are in and out of money. When broke, they hang on the rail bordering the poker pit and put the arm on the regulars for a stake. Many have a sweet tooth for other casino games like craps, and blow their money as soon as they get it. Others make a good living as part of a team, they squander it playing on their own. Only a few crank it out year in and year out—and they work for it. With agents stationed in every card-room, they get a phone call whenever a "live one" pulls up a chair. Within minutes they arrive, filling the vacant seats. Those whose network is less efficient wait, like birds of carrion, missing the main feast but hovering patiently to pick the bones clean.

Only a coveted few never seem to be out of money. One of these is Hot Dog Willy. Willy comes from Brooklyn. Fourteen years ago he set out by bus to see the country and one of the stops was Las Vegas. Willy ambled into the Stardust Hotel and fell into a poker game. The bus left, but not Willy. Clad in a light blue sports jacket, faded yellow shirt, honeydew green pants with red suspenders, brown sox, black shoes, and a golf cap, Willy stayed on. A small, mousy-looking man with a waddling gait, Willy never looked back. He beat the pants off the fellas. Fourteen years later he still wears the same outfit. He has *never* been out of action. Although he keeps a low profile, he is estimated to have won more than $1,000,000. He acquired his nick-name "Hot Dog" because of the enormous quantity of frankfurters he has consumed over the years. Being a frugal man, Willy has taken advantage of the free sand-wiches afforded players by the casinos—and Willy loves hot dogs. There's no telling how many dogs he has con-sumed. Rumor has it that in fourteen years Willy has never eaten a meal outside the poker rooms! That's a lot of wieners!

Other big winners include Meredith Angel. Angel, as his wife affectionately calls him, fits the bill of a Mis-sissippi gambler par excellence. A product of Texas, he drawls as well as he plays. He will play any game you want for as much as you want. Two-handed or eight-

handed—makes no difference—Angel comes to play.
Big action? The bigger the better. I have heard that
Angel has come away with $1,000,000 in a single eve-
ning playing lowball. The stakes were reportedly
$16,000 before the draw, and $32,000 after. No, money
doesn't scare him off. He's got a lot of gamble in him.

One day Angel had to deliver a large sum of money
in cash to northern Nevada. He was accompanied by a
known "hit" man who would rub out a man for pocket
money. Angel delivered the loot without incident. When
he returned to Vegas, a friend asked, "Weren't you
nervous carrying all that dough with such a dangerous
man around?" "Well," Angel drawled, "I figured I'd
just as soon know where he was at all times. That way
I could kinda keep an eye on him." That's Angel. He's
still alive, still droll, and still holding down a seat in the
big games in Las Vegas.

Every year the Horseshoe Casino in downtown Las
Vegas hosts the world championships of poker. Players
from all over the country congregate, some for the
tournament, but most for the side action. The town is
loaded with games, and the shrewd player looks for a
soft spot. The premier event of the Championships is a
$10,000 buy-in, winner take all, "hold-'em" game.
Each player gets two cards, then five cards are placed
in the center of the table. These five are common cards
in all hands. The outcome is decided by the two cards
each player is "holding," hence the name, "hold-'em."
This tournament has been won by many of the big
names—Johnny Moss, Amarillo Slim, Pug Pearson—
all have won. This is a battle for the superpros and the
cream of the game always comes to the top. It takes
days before one player has all the money, and the stakes
are raised periodically to keep up the pace. Stamina,

skill, and a good bit of con are necessary to pull off this yearly biggy, and it has gained nationwide attention. How does the hometown champion rate in this field? To quote Amarillo Slim, "Sure, they've got a chance to win like anybody else. Course, I don't look for 'em to. You don't know what kind-a hand they're goin' to show you. Why, they might stay for all bets, then show you a white blackbird." Slim's right. The stranger doesn't stand much chance in the Championships.

A key ingredient, common to most of the pros, is a lot of con. If you have ever seen an interview with Amarillo Slim, you'll know what I mean. Long and thin, he swaggers beneath an ever-present Stetson hat. He plays the role of a hick cowboy from Amarillo, Texas, and this image has taken him a long way. He looks one down, but you'll have to get up early if you hope to get the best of him.

Some of these con men go to elaborate lengths to set up a pigeon. Hot Springs, Arkansas, used to be Mecca for underground gambling. A couple of Vegas sharpies arrived there under separate cover and got involved in a high-stakes, two-handed poker game with each other. The southern regulars smelled a rat and avoided the game. The two played on and on. For seventy-two straight hours they locked horns. Unkempt and bleary-eyed, they pressed on, seemingly oblivious to their surroundings. Finally the locals cracked. They became believers. No one would go through seventy-two hours of hell in a straight-backed chair just to put over a con. They were wrong. The sharks cleaned up!

Poker capers are elaborately conceived. A polished huckster may spend an entire evening baiting his prey. I was playing in a no-limit seven-card stud game. One of the players had a rather subtle tell. He would place his hole cards neatly on top of each other when he had an ace in the hole; otherwise his hole cards remained in random disarray. As the evening wore on, I noticed this pattern. At least one other player also had noticed it, as he made several exceptional plays, indicating to me that he, too, had picked up on the tell. Late in the evening a hand came up involving these two players. The first player (A) slid his hole cards together in a neat pile; the other (B) noticed. Player A had a king up, B a 10. As the hand progressed, the pot swelled to $3,000. A had nearly $5,000 left in front of him; B about twice that amount. When all the cards had been dealt, their boards looked like this:

(A) — K Q J 6 / XXX (hole cards)

(B) — 10 9 2 9 / XXX

B studied his hole cards. They were 7, 10, 9—a full house. He peered at A's board. Knowing A had neatly boxed his hole cards, B guessed that at least one of his opponent's hole cards was an ace. He put A on an ace high straight. No matter, so long as A had an ace in the hole, B couldn't lose. B led, betting $2,000. A paused. He looked nervous. Fidgeting with his chips for long minutes, his anxiety seemed on the rise. At last, with a desperate gesture, he pushed *all* his chips into the pot, calling the $2,000 and raising $3,000. Now it was B's turn to sweat. He was nobody's fool and took a moment to analyze the situation. His competitor was losing about $2,000. All night long he had tipped his hidden aces. Would he bet everything on a straight? Probably, he reasoned. This would give him a chance to get even and it would take a full house (which

B had) to beat him. The only worry B had was a
higher full house or four of a kind, and that chance
seemed remote. Finally B called. To his amazement, A
flipped over a full house—kings over jacks. The whole
thing had been one big con. A's tell with aces was a set-
up. When he knew his little quirk had been spotted, he
sprung the trap. B's jaw hung open with surprise. He
knew he had been tricked but could do nothing about
it. Shortly thereafter A quit. He had won nearly $5,000,
all at B's expense. I felt fortunate that I had not been
the sacrificial lamb. I must confess, I would have played
B's hand exactly as he had.

Wheelchair Bill, as the name indicates, is a para-
plegic confined to a wheelchair. He has had some
muscle atrophy in his arms and consequent coordination difficulties. One night Bill got tangled up with a
group of polished experts. They were playing no-limit
five-card stud. Bill was getting butchered as each of the
players took a piece out of him. The player to his left
really had his way with poor Bill. It was as if he was
looking at Bill's hole card. He was, in fact, doing just
that. As Bill awkwardly peeked at his hole card it would
flash, giving his observant opponent a quick glimpse. It
was all he needed to just run over luckless Bill. After
several hours a big hand came up. Bill had ace, 6, 6, Q
showing. The opponent to his left showed K, 7, 9, 4. He
had another king in the hole, giving him a pair of kings.
As usual, Bill had flashed his hole card—the spade 4.
Knowing he had a cinch, his opponent made a very
large bet. Duly hesitating, Bill called and raised everything he had. His opposition knew he was bluffing. After
all, he had *seen* the spade 4. Blithely he called, flipped
over a king, and started to drag the pot. Bill stuttered:
"Wait a minute," and clumsily flopped up the ace of

spades. "But that's impossible," blurted his bewildered adversary. He grabbed the deck. Everything was in order. The game broke up. Cagey old Bill had given his rival the once-over-lightly. In his room, before the game, he had carefully clipped the corner off the 4 of spades of one of his decks. He spent the rest of the night setting up his ploy. When he finally got a pair of aces back to back, he adroitly slipped the corner over the ace and carelessly exposed it for a moment. His target never stood a chance. Bill had him. His opponent left in disgust, kicking himself for having misread Bill's hand, since aces and 4's look similar.

Con men can take many forms. A doctor friend of mine was invited to a big out-of-town home game. After an hour's plane ride, no one met him at the airport. With much effort he finally tracked down the game's host. He was informed that all the seats had been filled, but he could come and watch, and if anyone split early, he was welcome to take his place. The game was held at a magnificent estate, and a spread of delicacies had been prepared. Excusing himself, the doctor made a trip to the men's room, slipping back unnoticed. Twenty minutes later the host got deathly ill. He paled and made a beeline for the toilet, retching violently. Apologizing profusely, he was forced to leave the game and offered my friend his seat. After a cursory examination of his host, the doctor sat down, and copped a very respectable win. The occasion of the host's malaise was precipitated by ipecac in his coffee. This harmless medication is used to induce vomiting in children who have swallowed some noxious substance. The doctor carried it routinely in his emergency kit. With its help, he had no trouble opening up a seat—an altogether devilish scheme.

In sum, Vegas poker is no haven for the amateur.

But for those readers who want to try their hand, Table 10 lists the casinos that host games and a summary of what you are likely to encounter.

TABLE 10

Location	Comments
Downtown casinos	Rake prohibitive in small-limit games. Grind joints. Repetitive field often tough. Rooms generally well managed. Top limit $10 & $20 and occasional no-limit games.
Sahara	Rake fair. Cheapest rake on Strip. Good management and playing conditions. Player generally protected. Top limit $30 & $60 seven-card high stud.
Stardust	Rake twenty-five percent of pots in small games. Fair rake in higher limit. Atmosphere raucous. Management spotty. Player on his own for protection, depending on shift. Top limit $15 & $30 seven-card high stud or low stud.
Flamingo	Small games unplayable due to rake. Features hold 'em, lowball, high-low split, seven-card high, and seven-card low. Will play anything you'll play and as high as you want. Player strictly on his own, especially after 2:00 A.M.
Caesar's Palace	New, beautiful facility. Five percent rake in small games. Generally fair rakes. Live games. Adequate protection. May be best "sleeper" for visitor. Top limit $20 & $40 seven-card high.

Location	Comments
MGM	Rake too high in low limit. Rake okay in $3 & $6 and $5 & $10. Very live games. All seven-card high. Tough local players in $5 & $10. $3 & $6 best action and least competition. Top limit $5 & $10.
Dunes	Rake too high in small games. Features high limit. Up to $200 & $400 seven-stud for high or low. Occ. $600 limit 2–7 lowball. Most consistent big game in town. Beware! Player *strictly* on his own. Tourist unlikely to win a ruling if controversy arises. Mid-priced ($15 & $30) often very lucrative (more so than Stardust). Only most competent should tackle big games.
Tropicana	All small games. Nothing inspirational here.
Hacienda	Small games. Tough to make a living.
Circus	Small games. Rake very low. Good spot for small-limit player. Good management. Might find a gift horse here.

13

For Women

BLACKJACK

Accentuate the Positive

Natural camouflage—their femininity—has provided women with the ability to become highly successful twenty-one players. Women automatically establish a complementary relationship with the exclusively male casino management. Male players must devote considerable attention to establishing warm, compatible relationships while assiduously avoiding competitiveness and power struggles. Women, on the other hand, are well received from the outset. Casino representatives at all echelons lower their guard and begin to covet the affections of the fairer sex. They naturally fall into the role of wooing, rather than defending. Getting back to the wolf analogy for a moment, the male wolf defends his territory against a male intruder. But a female intruder is actively sought after and, it is to be hoped, charmed into staying. These sexual roles aptly apply to a strange female entering the casino lair. The inhabitants of the gambling den will curiously sniff the alien female and, if finding her alluring, will actively pursue her in quest of her favors. A clever woman can fan these early sparks of desire and keep them smoldering. She is cautiously flirtatious and extremely feminine, accentuating her assets and minimizing her deficiencies. The courtship has begun and the astute female player is well on her way toward winning a fortune. She can have the dealer, pit boss, and executives all eating out of her hand, while carefully avoiding rivalries among her suitors. At every turn she remains sensual and provocative, soft, warm, and sensitive. She will find acceptance easy. Her entourage of casino personnel will actually go out of its way to facilitate her winning. Remember, Las Vegas is operating on the lower levels of human need—money, sex, and power. These needs are strong motivators for the locals. An attractive woman immediately strikes a sympathetic chord in the sex department. The door is wide open for the would-be female counter, and some are starting to take advantage of their built-in calling card.

April is one of this new breed of female player. At five-feet-one and ninety-eight pounds, she looks like a Kewpie doll. She radiates freshness, with rosy cheeks and bright blue eyes. She is vivacious, bubbly, and her petite nose wrinkles up like a rabbit's when she laughs. Although pushing thirty, she still is frequently asked for her I.D. at bars, her girlish looks belying her age. This picture of innocence is a superb twenty-one player! And with the help she gets from dealers and pit bosses, she is a 10-to-1 favorite to win every time she plays!

I met April two years ago in Lake Tahoe. She used to deal blackjack, but had given it up to become a player. She bet $5 to $25, averaging $100 per day. One day she slid into the chair next to me while I was playing. The dealer directed her attention to the $100-minimum sign at the table. She turned to me, eyes pleading, her mouth pursed in a slight pout, and asked me if I would really mind if she played with me. Like many others, I fell into her trap. She looked so hurt and so cute that I had to laugh, my frustration at the interruption rapidly melting. Her nose wrinkled as she giggled, and I had company. But before long my amusement changed to bewilderment. She played perfectly, and within minutes had the pit boss peeking at the dealer's hole card, advising her when to hit and stand. She won $150 while I lost $1,000, and, patting me affectionately on the hand, thanked me for allowing her to play and rose to go. I left too, inviting her to have a drink. "Sure," she said, "you were nice enough to let me play. I'm buying. After all, I'm the big winner," she said with a wink. She was quite guarded about her expertise, but when I opened up first, she responded with alacrity. With the ebullience of a child she explained how she had learned to play blackjack from her old boyfriend, a computer wizard. Together they worked on the blackjack program that she packaged into her pixie style. She practiced counting when she was dealing, and when she had it down pat, quit her job and started playing. She proudly told me that she had made nearly $10,000 in six months and had taken a lot of time off to enjoy life. She lauded the merits of being her own boss and making her own hours. She found this new freedom exhilarating.

I asked April if she had ever been to Las Vegas. She said she hadn't but was just about ready to make a trip. I told her I was on my way there and asked if she would accompany me. I also volunteered to stake her play. We struck a bargain and off we went.

April was just perfect for Vegas. Her cheerleader appearance caught them off guard and in no time she had the old-time casino hands laughing with her. Once again the dealers and pit bosses bent over backward to help her, despite her $100 and $200 bets. During her ten-day stay, she averaged $500 per hour! April had hit the big time! In ten days, her share of the winnings came to nearly $10,000. In a scant ten days she had equaled her earnings of the past six months. Now, adequately financed, she ventured off on her own. Since her Las Vegas debut, I have run into April several times. Each time, she had stacks of green $25 chips in front of her, her face alive with that impish grin, charming her willing hosts.

April typifies the selective advantage women have over men as twenty-one players. Not that a woman must fit into a girlish mold but, rather, she must accentuate and display her feminine characteristics. I have seen other expert female players flaunt different sides of the feminine mystique. One well-endowed woman I know wore dramatic clinging low-cut dresses, completely snapping the concentration of even the most dedicated pit boss. Another projected quiet elegance and sophistication—an exquisite, refined lady of means, who regularly beat the casinos out of $1,500 a day. One matron I know mothered the help into submission. She is a middle-aged, very well-rounded Italian lady, sharp as a tack. She is a solid blackjack player, yet, to a man, the casino help love her! They affectionately call her "Mama." Mama babies them constantly, cooing and clucking. Patiently she listens to their problems, freely giving advice, gently admonishing them when appropriate. They treat her with respect, almost reverence, and seem overjoyed at her consistent small wins. Mama never plays very high, content with a hundred or so a day. She enjoys her casino relationships, and the mother image is obviously a natural, easy role for her. The potential for the female player is limitless! Her sex alone puts her beyond suspicion, and the paucity of skilled female players dramatically adds to her disguise.

I know only one female player that has been barred —and you have to look twice to be certain she is female. This woman does everything possible to eliminate her feminine traits. She dresses in jeans and a man's work shirt. She wears no makeup, and her unkempt hair is closely cropped. She sports a short, muscular body. Her gait is the envy of every rodeo champion. Her mannerisms at the table are brusque, and she swears vehemently when she loses. It's no wonder she makes the hair on the back of the pit boss's neck bristle. She manages to invite confrontation and eventually gets it. In the eyes of the casino she is similar to a defiant male counter, and the relationship is one of symmetrical confrontation, climaxing with expulsion. But apart from this notable exception, no woman has been barred! Yet I know only four competent female players. Why?

Pitfalls

Fear is the most inhibiting factor. Many women I have talked with lack confidence that they can win. The role of a gambler is alien to most women and carries with it the burden of fear of the unknown.

For those who get beyond this fear, other pitfalls await. Playing twenty-one is a discipline. Both mind and body are strained by the circumstances. Money and risk are involved, and emotions tend to run high. Most women react to stress more emotionally than men. Superstition and intuition run higher, and they may rely more on hunches than sound strategy. Women seem to take losses harder than men and their confidence is more easily shaken. They are particularly susceptible to mood swings prior to their menstrual periods. These factors compound the difficulty in maintaining control and discipline, especially in the face of adverse circumstances, such as the inevitable losing streaks. Some budding female players have their confidence shaken early in their careers, and give up prior to becoming proficient. The female players I have known need constant support and encouragement, but who doesn't? Many a woman is squelched by the man in her life and discouraged from playing. Many men are threatened by competency of any kind in their women, especially when her earning power exceeds his.

But given proper support, maximizing their God-given attributes, and maintaining composure, women are a lead-pipe cinch to win, and to continue winning indefinitely.

One of my long-range goals is to train and finance a flock of attractive, finely tuned female counters and descend on Las Vegas en masse. The results would be devastating. Like a swarm of locusts, the females would devour the crop of money and the casinos wouldn't even know what hit them.

Some Helpful Hints

If you are a female player, you must walk a fine line for maximum effectiveness. You must discover the casino power structure and play up to the chiefs without offending the Indians. You should be pleasant, but reserved with the other customers. Although flirtatious with the help, you must avoid consummating relationships, as this is certain to lead to trouble. Las Vegas is a back-stabbing community, and if knowledge of your relationship with an "insider" leaks, you will immediately become suspect. Small tokens of affection will be lapped up by your courters. Give a boss a flower for his lapel and watch him beam with satisfaction, like a knight bearing the colors of his lady. Or make a small handmade gift or card for some of the boys in appreciation for their kindness. Personalized gifts are much more effective than tipping—and far less expensive. Try not to slight anyone, even if you find someone distasteful.

One of the more serious problems you will encounter is in northern Nevada. Here the dealers are predominantly female and the pit bosses exclusively male. In this situation it is easy to become catty and competitive with the dealers, vying for the attentions of the pit bosses. The female–female relationship is similar to the male–male dynamic, and you may threaten the dealer. You must carefully avoid this potential conflict. Interact directly with the female help and treat them as peers. Be complimentary and seek their aid and advice. Remember, enemies of either sex can be expensive!

Playing with Male Partners

Mixed doubles is becoming popular around the twenty-one circuit. Many capable male players, put off by the constant pressure, have taken in a female partner. A couple arouses considerably less suspicion than a man playing alone. Some pairs use signals for making playing decisions, while others make independent decisions, both players being equally competent.

Recently I spoke with a highly talented pair who

strongly advocated this approach. Years ago, the man had been hassled for counting. The woman had met with frustration and lost control when she tried playing solo. But together they were dynamite! They had worked out a routine to minimize suspicion and maximize gain. The plan was simple. The man would make small bets, never betting more than $10 on a hand. The woman bet $50 to $200. They worked out a set of knee signals for consultation purposes. He kept an accurate count for insurance bets (counting 10's), while she used a plus-minus count for betting and playing decisions. They told me they were enjoying handsome gains with unbelievably few hassles. They say that couple play, with the woman doing the serious betting, goes over the heads of the pit bosses, significantly reducing the risk of detection. They are playing about an hour a day and averaging $2,000 a week!

POKER

The psychological tactics in poker are entirely different from those in blackjack. In blackjack, you must ingratiate yourself to be able to continue playing. You have a strong advantage and if allowed to play, will certainly win. Poker, on the other hand, is a contest between individuals. The reality of poker is conflict. In blackjack you go out of your way to avoid confrontation, in poker you create it. Poker is a game of balance. The more off balance you can keep your opponents, the greater your chances of winning. Upsetting traditional role relationships is an outstanding way to disturb an opponent's balance, and, once again, women have the inside track. Flirtation and seductiveness are out of place here, as these affectations are familiar to the male players and it is easy for them to cope, remaining centered. What traits in a woman will throw her male opponents out of kilter? Those which he least expects and least likes—aggressiveness, assertiveness, strength, and decisiveness.

Most men react strongly to female aggression. Many poker players are quite "macho" and don't think any woman can play well. Compound this deeply ingrained conditioning with contentious behavior, and the Marlboro man goes berserk! I have seen competent male poker players run amok in the face of female aggression. They rise to the challenge and feel compelled to suppress the female upstart.

One night in Las Vegas I witnessed a confrontation between six men and a lone woman. As if defending their sex, the men ganged up on the intruder. She rose to the challenge, responding with aggressive play and combative demeanor. The men seemed obsessed with putting this maverick back in her place. She kept egging them on and they blindly plunged into pot after pot in their attempts to squelch her. The more she refused to submit, the harder they pushed. It was obvious to me that they were totally out of control and, worse yet, had no defense. Their conditioning was too strong, their actions involuntary. At the end of the evening all six men were losers and the woman made off with over $10,000! Even after she left, they continued to grumble over how a woman who can't play worth a lick could walk away with all the money. They were powerless, completely caught up in an unconscious response.

Conditions are changing for female poker players. Until recently, most of them were patsies—rich women throwing away money out of boredom. Most were not playing their own money, but blowing what their husbands gave them. A new breed of female player is emerging. As women become more liberated, some of them are applying their newly found assertiveness to the poker table with formidable results. Abandoning their traditionally submissive role, they are fomenting conflict and winding up with all the marbles. I predict you will see, in the years to come, a rapidly increasing number of winning professional female poker players. The male pro, so long the dominant figure in these games, had best become liberated himself if he hopes to stand a chance.

14

Cheating

When people and money come together, the temptation to abscond with a little of the loot is overwhelming. Some people are easily overwhelmed and, with little aplomb, brazenly steal what they can. Others spend years learning the subtle art of thievery, interminably practicing techniques to elude the wary eyes of the casino security network. They have to go some to fool these sharpies, who have been raised on gambling and nurtured on the tricks of the trade. Sophisticated electronic equipment helps them monitor each game. Television cameras stationed above each table are equipped with special lenses that can zoom in on a game and clearly pick up the hairs on the back of a player's hands! Electronic eyes watch the cashier's cage, and plainclothes detectives roam the aisles. Some casinos hire detective agencies specializing in gambling. Their agents are thoroughly trained in all the variations of cheating, theft, embezzlement, and graft. They know what to look for and how to snare even the most cautious thief. Their tentacles spread to all parts of the casino and encompass player, dealer, pit boss, and executive. Inquisitive, they scan everyone. Their sensitive tendrils are triggered by the subtlest impropriety, and everyone is suspect. They seem to be able to sense a difference in the air when a rip-off is in progress, and with unerring efficiency, zero in on the source. But despite all these precautions, the casinos are ripped off daily! People are constantly inventing new, more elaborate schemes to slip through the casino security net. The depth and extent of this ingenuity is truly formidable. And so this game of catch-if-catch-can goes on, a microcosm within the world of glittering lights and mink coats.

BLACKJACK

Marking Cards

At first blush it would appear that there is little a player can do to cheat at twenty-one. The dealer shuffles and deals, the player only coming in contact with two or three cards a hand. The dealer is only a foot or two away, backed up by a couple of hawk-eyed pit bosses, so cheating must be impossible. Wrong! For the slick pro, touching two cards at a time is enough. Marking the cards is the most common form of chicanery. This may be accomplished by simply crimping the cards. Holding the card between thumb and forefinger, a quick squeeze creates a slight wave in the card. Now, instead of lying flush on the table, part of the card is slightly elevated to the trained eye of the cheat. Usually he selects the 10's as the object of his art. Knowing when the dealer has a 10 in the hole or when the top card is a 10 is an enormous advantage. Only the most skilled and perceptive pit bosses can detect the subtle alterations made by these experts.

Cards can also be marked by using daub. Daub leaves an almost invisible smudge on the cards. It comes in several forms, the best varieties being extremely difficult to detect by any save the artist who applies them. One night in Las Vegas I watched a command performance by two virtuoso daubers. The female of the duo was quite attractive, with long blond hair cascading down her back. Perched pertly on the stool, she charmed both dealer and pit boss with disarming smiles. She chattered incessantly, betting $5 on each hand. But all the while she sat there, her hands were busy. With the quickness and expertise of a concert pianist, her fingers played over the back surfaces of the cards. Tens she gently touched twice, at the top and bottom of the card. Deuce, 3, 4, 5, and 6 were graced only once (on a corner). Aces were fondled at the center. Her graceful fingers would flit from the cards to the small hollow behind her right earlobe where the daub was neatly concealed by lobe and flowing hair. Back and forth from ear to card her knowing fingers moved, until the entire deck was marked. Enter her partner, distinguished, graying, nattily attired in Beverly Hills sportswear. He sauntered over to the table, casually occupying the seat next to the lady (until now cleverly occupied by her purse to dissuade intruders).

Then the fireworks started. The new addition began playing for $100 a hand and up. His play was astounding. Sometimes he would stay on 12 against a 10, other times he would hit 15 against a 6 (as when he knew the dealer had an ace in the hole). He won steadily, leaving after about half an hour with nearly a $5,000 profit. Shortly thereafter his partner softly said her good-bys, bemoaning her $50 loss. To avoid the remote possibility of detection they were careful to leave before the deck was changed. Vegas contacts of mine tell me the polished pair have pulled this caper all over the world without being caught. *Bonne chance!*

Another ingenious technique for marking cards is the application of paint visible only through specially designed contact lenses. Here the practitioner can proceed unmolested, since detection requires first, suspicion, then equally elaborate countermeasures.

Holding Out

One of the most artful forms of cheating involves sleight of hand. Like the master magician, years of practice allow the expert to deceive his audience (in this case, the casino management). Several variations are popular, the most common being the holdout artist who removes an ace from the table by hiding the card in his palm. He then substitutes it for another card at the appropriate moment, and voilà—blackjack! A professional holdout man can move cards in and out so quickly and with such proficiency that detection is exceedingly difficult even when you know what he is doing and are looking for it. Some of these manual wizards can remove two to three cards and fashion whatever hand they choose—sometimes a double down, sometimes a blackjack—and always with an air of total calm and nonchalance. Naturally, their reward and risk are commensurate with their skill. Their biggest risk comes when the decks are changed. Decks are always counted by a pit boss and if he finds cards missing, the jig is up. The masters take a few risks, removing cards shortly after a new deck is installed, and putting them back long before the deck is replaced.

Cheating

Switching Cards

Wouldn't you like to be able to play two hands, be allowed to look at both, then move the cards around as you pleased? For example, if you are dealt 10/6 on the first hand and ace/5 on the second, you could exchange the 6 for the ace, giving you blackjack and 11. Some people do just that! A counter friend of mine was playing in Reno. A middle-aged couple was innocuously playing for $10–$20 a hand. Out of the corner of his eye the counter noticed a most curious event. He glimpsed a 16, then moments later saw the matron turn over a blackjack! The 6 joined a 5 in her partner's hand and he doubled down. And it all happened so fast and so smoothly, the counter thought his eyes were deceiving him. But no, it was true! On several other occasions he observed similar exchanges. The couple was so practiced at this move that, try as he might, he could not see the actual switch being made. He would get a peek at one hand and in a blink it would become another. To add insult to injury, the casino management asked *him* to leave because he was counting while, expressionless, the couple proceeded undisturbed.

Another dowdy couple pulled off a similar caper in Las Vegas. A printer friend of theirs duplicated cards from every casino in town. Then they went to play, armed with this formidable arsenal. The woman played and the man stood behind her, adroitly supplying her with the card she needed. A quick hit, then on to the next joint. Rumor has it they were finally discovered when he accidentally slipped a Stardust card into a Riviera deck. Whoops!

161

Replacing Cards

Not very long ago in Las Vegas, and still common in other parts of the world, the used cards were placed in untopped, two-sided plastic receptacles. It didn't take long for the cheats to spot an opportunity here. Clearly, it would be advantageous to remove some small cards from play and substitute 10's and aces in their place. So they did. While one member of the scam team distracted the dealer and pit boss responsible for the game, another quickly dropped half a dozen 10's or aces into the open discards. Then, as play continued, they would remove an equal number of small cards from play. Then repeat the procedure. They would focus their attention on four-deck games, so no one raised an eyebrow when two heart aces appeared in the same hand. Also, shoes are only changed once a shift, so they had eight full hours to enjoy the fruit of their labor. Once set up, other team members would come in and play during the shift, each winning a bundle and leaving. Only when the shift ended and the decks were sorted would the casino realize it had been swindled. In Las Vegas plastic tops have been added to the card receptacles for protection, but it's still open season in Europe and other parts of the world for these poachers.

Knowing the Dealer's Hole Card

Knowing the dealer's hole card gives the player about an eleven percent advantage. A lot of cheating hinges on a knowledge of the dealer's cards. The simplest way to get this information is for the dealer or pit boss to tip off the player after the dealer has looked at his down card. Dealer-player or pit boss-player partnerships exist, and elaborate signals are used to transmit the desired information. Profits are shared.

When insiders are not involved, the proposition is a bit more difficult. Some dealers are sloppy when they peek at their hole card, raising it unshielded. A sharp eye can see it from the other side of the blackjack pit, some ten feet away. The observer then signals his partner. Since pit bosses are often tuned in to this kind of trickery and are wary of an observer who scratches his nose or adjusts his glasses too often, some more sophisticated signaling schemes have been devised. One of the most sophisticated employs an electronic device, the receiving end strapped to the player's leg. The sender signals by means of tiny electric shocks that the player can feel on his leg, indicating the dealer's exact hole card. Some casinos now have electronic detection systems to help uncover the use of these signaling devices.

Dealer-Player Partnerships

One of the most common forms of cheating is collusion. Since the dealer is so closely watched by supervisors, hidden cameras, and house security, out-and-out pilferage is next to impossible. But if the dealer can make it easier for a player to win and share in his profits, discovery is far less likely. Tipping his hole card to his player-partner has already been discussed. On occasion, the player may add chips to his bet *after* looking at his hand, or the dealer may knowingly overpay a winning hand.

More cunning are card manipulation schemes. Some dealers can perform wonders with a deck of cards. Known as "mechanics," they "fix" the cards as they choose, changing the natural distribution. The most common technique is called "peeking." When a dealer collects or pays a bet, he must turn over the hand holding the deck. The deck is now upside down, with the top card closest to the table. Now, imperceptibly, the dealer squeezes the lower left-hand corner of the deck, "peeking" at the corner of the top card. If it's a 10 or an ace, he deals normally, giving it to his partner. But if it is a small card, he moves it sideways, ever so slightly, and deals the *second card* to his partner, saving the small card for himself.

In the old days, when Las Vegas was run by the mob, mechanics were hired to "protect the house." Such protection was sometimes needed when a high roller got exceptionally lucky, or when a counter needed to be taught a financial lesson. Now, with tighter gaming control, house mechanics are extremely rare. But some of these slick operators have gone into business for themselves, throwing hands to their player-partner. To avoid detection, they strive to get back the money they dished out to the unsuspecting tourist, especially the big player. Each table in Las Vegas is closely monitored by management. If one table consistently does worse than the others, it becomes suspect. If a dealer is throwing off, say, $1,000 a day to his partners, this will eventually show up, so he protects himself by making sure he wins *more* from the other players. He may cheat unsuspecting players not on instruction from the house, but to cover himself by compensating for losses to his partner. Needless to say, such renegade dealers are frowned upon by the casinos and, when discovered, are blackballed from dealing anywhere, ever again.

Sometimes elaborate schemes are conjured up involving players, dealers, and pit bosses. One caper recently unfolded at a large Strip hotel. Two men and a woman played against a shoe. When the dealer handed the woman the cards to cut, she deftly swept them into her oversized purse, replacing them with four identical-looking prearranged decks. The pit boss and dealer conveniently looked away while this happened. Now the trio played against the set-up shoe, won a bundle, and split. The scheme was finally detected, but there is no telling how much damage this team inflicted on the casino coffers. Just prior to being apprehended, they had won $22,000!

The greatest percentage of pilferage, by far, involves "insiders," like the dealer and pit boss in the caper just mentioned. Outright theft (pocketing chips directly) is exceedingly difficult with modern electronic surveillance. Most schemes require the cooperation of two or more persons. The combination of pit boss, dealer, and player-agent is potentially the most dangerous to the casino. Tipping the hole card, "coolers" (stacked decks), incorrect payoffs, and dumping to a player are all easiest with this combination.

Sometimes the marker system may be abused. A player with credit comes in and asks for $2,000. The dealer gives him the chips, but the player doesn't sign the marker. The player makes a few token bets, then leaves with the $2,000. There is no record of the $2,000 debit. The player, dealer, and pit boss cut up the $2,000. Normally the pit boss is the check on the dealer, and the dealer the check on the pit boss, but when they are in cahoots, the system obviously fails. Naturally, casino management is constantly figuring out ways to close loopholes, but there is always someone around figuring out new flaws, trying to make an easy buck.

Markers may also be falsified. A player may come in and ask his pit boss partner for $2,000. He is given a marker to sign, but instead of $2,000, a zero is conveniently omitted. The marker for $200 is signed and recorded. The extra $1,800 is split up. There are numerous variations on this theme, involving pit boss, dealer, and player in various combinations. Naturally, some are more clever than others, making detection difficult. Others are more transparent and the cheats are quickly apprehended.

If it seems that I have been lauding cheating in this chapter, I want to correct this misconception. I think any form of theft and cheating is deplorable. Some of these schemes are devilishly clever and inspire a certain amount of awe. I often wonder about the results such ingenuity would yield if legitimately directed. There are many games that can be beaten (such as twenty-one), and it seems that those capable of such feats of chicanery would be eminently capable of winning without jeopardizing their careers.

POKER

Wherever poker is played, the possibility of cheating exists. Marked cards are one of its most popular forms. Anyone who has played a lot of poker will at times notice small flaws, specks, food stains, or bends in a well-used deck of cards. There is nothing illegal about using your powers of perception to identify markings from natural causes. But sometimes the markings are not accidental, and even worse, are often undetectable to all but their creator.

A professional poker player I know had a regular weekly high-stakes poker game at his house. He made a handsome living off the game and quickly eliminated cheaters. One night a stranger stopped by and started winning at a rapid pace. Some of his decisions alerted the host's expert eye. It soon became apparent that the newcomer was daubing the cards. Since the game was seven-card high stud, the stranger was marking the high cards—jack, queen, king, and ace. His system was simple. Aces were smudged in one corner, kings in two, queens three, and jacks in all four. As soon as the host was certain of the marking system, he excused himself momentarily, then returned. Several hands later he was dealt an ace in the hole. As expected, one corner bore a barely perceptible smudge. Quickly the host reached down to his belt, obtaining a bit of daub he had hidden during his brief absence, and smeared a second corner of the card. It was now marked like a king. In similar manner he marked kings as queens, and queens as jacks. Jacks he left untouched. The net effect was that there were now no cards marked as aces and eight cards marked as jacks, all but the four real jacks now being mismarked. In a very short time the cheat realized he had been discovered and made a hurried exit. Next day the pro called the cheater at his office. The pro threatened to expose the man's cheating unless he promptly gave him his winnings. Since the other players were valued business associates of the cheater, he reluctantly agreed. He was never invited back.

Bending and Crimping

I'm sure you have seen some people bend cards when shuffling, or when "squeezing out" their hole card, thus elevating a corner of the card. This type of behavior is usually random and harmless—but not always. A crafty cheat can selectively bend cards that appear perfectly natural. This allows him to identify the hole cards of other players and to make his own playing decisions unerringly. He always knows when other players are bluffing and folds powerful hands, knowing when he is beat. Crimping is a variation of bending.

To protect yourself against this kind of manipulation, take the deck when it's your deal, Square it up, and place it firmly on the table. Now lower your eyes to the level of the deck. The cards should be resting one on top of the next with no spaces between. If you notice spaces between the cards, cut to that card and smooth out the waves so it once again rests flat. If the cards continue to arrive bent when it's your deal, notice the value of the bent cards. If a pattern develops, you probably have a cheat in the roost. If random, caution the other players that they are bending the cards and ask for a new deck.

Sanding, Shaving, and Painting

Sometimes cards are marked in advance. Since the artist has more time and no one is observing, this type of marking is more subtle and elaborate. Key cards may be shaved or sanded, removing a few millimeters of their surface. They are easily identified by the cheat when he deals. On occasion every card is marked. Line shade is a kind of paint applied along the natural markings or border of the cards. The length of the line indicates the denomination of the card.

The Cooler

Decks can be set up in advance. The cheat asks for a new deck when it's his deal and brings in the stacked deck, known as a "cooler." He then shuffles without disturbing the set-up hand and a few minutes later rakes in a huge pot.

Do not be fooled by decks that are sealed and wrapped in cellophane. Cheaters can arrange to have phony or marked decks sealed and wrapped. Whenever a new deck is brought out, ask to examine it. Fan it on both sides and closely examine the markings and borders. The cards should be in sequence, sorted by suit. If you notice anything amiss, play a few more token hands, then quietly excuse yourself.

Sleight of Hand

Undoubtedly you have seen magicians perform wonders with cards; these experts would be put to shame by some of the sharpies who sometimes frequent poker games. A friend of mine was playing draw poker in one of California's public poker palaces. An expert player, he became suspicious of one of the other players who was consistently winning. He watched him intently but could not observe anything out of line. The winner wasn't marking the cards and did not seem to be teamed up with any of the other players. The deal came around to my friend. As he shuffled, he examined the backs of the cards, observing nothing out of the ordinary. There was a total of eight players in the game. He dealt five cards to each. Five of the players folded. The first drew one card, the second and third drew two cards each. He had now dealt a total of forty-five cards. He should have had seven cards left undealt but, fanning the remaining cards, he counted only five. Two cards were missing! The fellow with all the chips was holding out cards, slipping them in when needed. But even knowing the method of cheating, my friend's skilled eye could not detect the move. Like a master magician, the cheat continued to move cards in and out undetected. The management was alerted to the presence of the cheat and his method, but could not catch him either and discounted the story. This cheat is still an active player in California cardrooms and has never been caught.

Holding out cards is the most frequent use of sleight-of-hand cheating. It is exceptionally hard to detect and very effective. As such, it is the most dangerous form of cheating in poker. It can be used in any poker game in the world and requires no prearrangement. You will find people capable of holding out in many big-money games. You may also find people capable of detecting these cheats in the same game. However, the cheats tend to avoid the pros, fleecing only the tourists and high rollers. Sometimes, when caught by a pro, the cheat will privately arrange to share his winnings with the pro in exchange for keeping the cheat's secret. Often the pro readily agrees.

Incredible sleight-of-hand feats can be performed by the expert while dealing. He can deal "seconds" or "bottoms." Instead of dealing the top card to the first player, the proficient dealer gives him the second card in the deck. This is accomplished by sliding the top card slightly to the left and, in the same motion, grasping the corner of the second card and sliding it out. This move can be done so quickly and smoothly that it can't be seen even by experts. Some say they can "hear" seconds being dealt. When a card is dealt in normal fashion, only the bottom surface comes in contact with the other cards. But when a second is dealt, both the top and bottom surfaces make contact with other cards. The result is a swishing sound from rubbing against two surfaces, a sound audible to the trained ear.

Like seconds, bottoms can be dealt without arousing suspicion. In this case the dealer deals himself or his partner the bottom card instead of the top card.

A key card—or an entire hand, for that matter—can be brought to the top with a shuffle. Cards can be shuffled and cut without changing the order. In short, the sleight-of-hand expert, known as a mechanic, can do just about anything he wants with a deck of cards without much risk of detection by an unsuspecting audience.

If all this leaves you incredulous, go to the Bacchanal Room at Caesar's Palace for the 9:30 P.M. seating. During dinner ask the maitre d' to have Jimmy Grippo come over and entertain you. While sipping your after-dinner drinks, you will be treated to the damnedest display of close-up sleight-of-hand magic you've ever seen. Jimmy's moves are flawless, and he moves cards in and out with lightning quickness. Defying you to catch him in the act, he will repeat tricks over and over, a mere foot or two away from you. When at last you give up, he informs you that he has lost some of the quickness of his youth. Falling for his trap, you observe his velvet-smooth, nimble hands, trim body, and perfect mental control. You ask, "How old are you?" He quietly informs you he was born in 1892! Now if a man of eighty-six still has the dexterity to pull the wool over your eyes time and time again, getting a deck of cards to do everything but talk, imagine what chance you have in a poker game against a sleight-of-hand expert. Jimmy will tell you he doesn't gamble and isn't allowed near a casino, but unfortunately there are others, maybe not quite so polished, but good enough to get the money.

*　　*　　*

Teams

Poker is a tough game when each person is on his own. When two or more gang up against the others, in the long run they will get the money, especially if they are decent players to boot. Poker teams are common in the public poker houses of California and Nevada. Sometimes you need a scorecard to keep track of which teams are in action. Teammates usually use a set of signals known as "offices." The types of signals used are limitless, but include the position of the cards, the position of the player's hand when looking at the cards, the way a player handles his chips, and verbal cues. Some teams operate by having the player with the best hand go after the pot. Others use "muscle" to rob antes.

Let's say you are playing draw poker in a California poker house. One player opens the pot, a second raises, now the action comes to you. You must call two bets to play, and can again be raised and reraised. Unless you have a high three-of-a-kind, you must fold. The team locks up the antes. In the course of an evening, stealing antes by a team can amount to a small fortune.

Teams also set traps for the unwary. When one team member has a powerhouse hand, he will signal his cohorts. Say you make a good hand and would call a bet after the draw. The team member to your right bets into you. You call. Then the man with the powerhouse raises and his teammate reraises. Now you must call two more bets. The team makes sure that the last raise is made by the powerful hand. If the last bet is called, the big hand is shown and the other team member quickly discards his hand. The other players only see the good hands.

Team players will try to see other players' hole cards

172

and signal their partners. Often, players unaware that a team is at work will freely show their cards to the player next to them. They may as well turn their cards face up! It is natural to become careless when the players around you have thrown away their hands. They have no interest in the pot, so they should be harmless enough. Beware! Unless you know all the players in the game, keep your hand hidden at all times, no matter how innocuous a game may seem.

A poker game is no place to relax. When you are not involved in a pot, keenly observe the activities of the other players. If bets seem strange or unusual, or if several players constantly seem to be raising one another, be especially vigilant. Watch the way they look at their cards, the position of their hands, the way they handle their chips, and any other movements, however subtle, that seem to fall into a pattern. The best way to handle a scam team is to discover their signals. If you are sharp enough, you may be able to decipher their entire code and know the *exact* hand of each team member. Now *they* are playing with their cards exposed and you are in position to clean up. You will always know exactly where you stand, so every decision you make will be totally accurate.

A well-known player, nicknamed Joker, was playing in a five-card draw game for low. Known as "California lowball," this is the most popular game in California. The best hand is A2345, next best A2346, then A2356, etc. The object is to get the *lowest* hand— that is the one closest to A2345. Early in the contest Joker smelled a rat. The game was fast and loose; all bets were $80. As Joker watched, he slowly saw a pattern emerge. The players in the first, fourth, and fifth seats were teamed up. They were using "muscle" to steal antes when none of them had a hand, and sometimes trapping players when one of them had the "nuts" (a near-perfect hand).

Joker zeroed in on the team and it wasn't long before he discovered their offices. He watched a little longer to confirm his suspicions, then took action. When the team would raise and reraise, signaling they had nothing, Joker would step right in and raise himself. One of the team would drop and the other would try to bluff his way through the hand. He would not draw, indicating a strong hand, but Joker just rapped pat right behind him. The cheat would check, but not Joker. With certainty he would bet out. Reluctantly his opponent would throw away his hand. When the team would signal power, Joker would drop out, avoiding the trap. After a couple of hours, Joker was winning $2,000.

One of the team suggested raising the stakes. Several of the other players, all losers, encouraged the idea, hoping to get even. Naturally, Joker, not one to disappoint the crowd, nodded approval. The stakes were doubled to $160 a bet. Joker continued to consistently outwit the scam team. Then an unusual thing happened. Joker was dealt A2346, the second-best possible hand. Casually he looked over to catch the signals. One of the team signaled that he had a 6 made for low. Joker knew the possible hands he could have were A2346, A2356, A2456, and A3456. Joker's hand tied the first of these and beat the other three. One of the team with a nothing hand bet into Joker. Knowing the power lay behind him, Joker called. On cue, the team member with the "duke" (a big hand is often referred to as a duke) raised. His teammate reraised. Joker merely called. The duke took the last raise. Call. Call. The nothing hand drew one; Joker and the other player stood pat. After the draw the empty hand again bet into Joker. Joker hesitated, then limped in, calling once again. Crash! The duke raised. His partner reraised. Joker called. Again a raise from the big hand. His partner put on an Academy-award performance, dropping out in mock disgust. Now Joker set the hook. He raised for the first time. When only two players remain in the pot, there is no limit on raises. The scam artist looked at Joker as if seeing him for the first time. Had he been sucked in? He tested Joker one more time with a raise. Joker, more quickly this time, reraised. A sick look materialized at the corners of the cheat's mouth. Slowly he called Joker's last bet. Joker showed him A2346. His opponent showed down A2356. Including antes, Jokers raked in an even $3,000! The game went on into the night. Shortly before morning the team dropped out, one by one. Joker had won over $11,000, his secret well guarded. The cheats hobbled off, wondering what had gone wrong.

If you pick up a set of offices in a poker game, use them to your best advantage. Don't feel obliged to report your findings to the cardroom management. The standard of ethics in poker does not require you to finger a cheat, especially if you can profit from your observations. Poker is a true example of the doctrine of "caveat emptor." Each player is responsible for himself and his decisions. The more observant and alert come out on top, the others fend as best they can.

Dealer Help

In some public poker games a dealer is provided by the house. Most house dealers are honest, but occasionally the dealer and a player will team up. The dealer may send his partner another player's hand, give him too much change, or manipulate the deck to benefit his partner. More rarely, he may bring in a marked deck. This type of cheating is extremely difficult to detect, especially if the dealer is a skilled "mechanic." The best way to handle this situation is to leave at the first hint of suspicion. There will be other games, so don't tolerate needless risks.

Railbirds

When playing poker, observe the "kibitzers" as well as the players. An apparently innocent bystander may be sending your hand over to another player. In Las Vegas a rail separates the poker tables from the main casino area. This rail is usually laden with observers. Most are curious tourists, but a few are agents paid to spy on other players' hands and tip off their partners.

Not long ago I walked into a well-known Las Vegas casino and a big poker game was in progress. The game was seven-card stud; the stakes $200 and $400. This means that on the first and second betting rounds all bets and raises are $200. On the third, fourth, and fifth betting rounds all bets and raises are $400. Playing were five seasoned pros and two very wealthy high rollers who were throwing the party. Like a pack of jackals, the locals tussled over how the prey would be divided. Two of the players were teamed up, but one look at the rail told the story. It looked like a macabre Greek chorus! Where'd they all come from? Behind each high roller lurked a dozen known hustlers. There was Shoeshine, Whitey, Ike, Toothpick, and Slick to name a few, all jockeying for position as if the Kentucky Derby were in progress: They were literally elbowing one another, vying for premier position. The high rollers were none too careful about concealing their hands, and the locals were cleaning up with the help of the vultures on the rail. It was really a comedy. Not once did the high rollers question why the kibitzers were all clustered behind *their* chairs. Perhaps it bolstered their egos. At any rate, the rest is history. When the smoke cleared, the pros had neatly cut up $70,000 and the party was over.

Stealing Chips

Some poker players will try to get the money any way they can, no holds barred. Some go directly to the source—the pot. After all, all that money in there really doesn't belong to anyone, so why not make off with a little? If a stray chip wanders in their direction, these shysters will, in one motion, palm the chip and neatly tidy up the pot for the other players. Another cute trick I've seen is exchanging a $5 chip for a $100 chip. Having already palmed a $5 chip from his stack, the cheat may grab a rolling $100 chip, effortlessly throwing the $5 chip in the pot. The other players see a chip fall into the mélange of other chips, but the exchange is done too quickly for them to catch the denomination.

Some are still more brazen. I was playing in Vegas one night and left momentarily to go to the rest room. I counted my chips before I left. When I returned, a $100 chip was missing from my stack. The balding, cigar-smoking player to my right was closest to the stack, but I had no evidence. Later I broached the incident with a poker pro acquaintance of mine. "Who, Slick?" he queried. "He does that all the time. Nicked you for a hundred, huh? Well, you gotta learn to protect your chips. Man's gotta make a living one way or another and Slick can't play poker. And you'd better cover up your hand real good if you see him on the rail. Gets paid pretty good for sending those hands over to his cronies." So I learned to protect myself. The best way to protect your chips when you leave the table is to take them with you. Failing that, cover each stack with three or four $1.00 chips or Eisenhower dollars. The thief must now dislodge the small stuff to get at the real money. This will usually attract the attention of the dealer and the other players. An uncovered stack is open invitation to steal.

Shorting Pots

When you make a bet, you would naturally like the calling players to put in the correct amount of money. Seems simple enough. But pot shorting is a very common form of cheating. Surprisingly, it is more prevalent in home games than in public ones. I cannot remember playing in a home game when there were no "errors" in bet amounts. Some of these are genuine oversights. Some are not. One pro I spoke with told me he averages $50 a day by shorting pots. "You've got to cover expenses," he explained. Players can short pots by not putting enough money in the pot, or by taking too much out when making change. A few shrewdies rob pots by palming chips when calling a bet or making change. Players can throw a variety of chips into the pot, making it impossible to tell how much they contributed.

To prevent pot shorting, demand that each player put his bet neatly in front of him. If any player varies from this, you have the right to stop the game and count the pot. If there is money missing, insist that the man who made the sloppy bet make the pot right. In a public game you can ask the dealer to reconcile the pot if you suspect pot shorting. Players who are not involved in the pot should not have their hands in it. If they want to make change, ask them to wait until the hand is over and you will gladly accommodate them.

I play in a regular weekly poker game. The first night I played, I noticed that two players were shorting pots. On that first night alone, one player made off with $50, the other with $100. For the next several weeks I carefully observed their antics. They were consistent. The first night was a representative sample. The two filched about the same amount each night. But what a difference in the way the two played! The $100 thief was an absolute dream. He dropped out of a pot only when he had no possible chance of winning, and even then he made a few mistakes. He stayed to the end ninety percent of the time. The limit was $50, so his pilferage only amounted to two bets. I would have gladly paid twice that every week just for the chance to play with such a nice player. If he needed a little token to bolster his spirits and lessen the pain of his mammoth losses, I felt a little peculation could be overlooked. The other player, however, was no bargain. He played tight and very slow. He was obese, had a positively repugnant personality, and was plagued with flatulence. He chilled the pace of the game, destroying the atmosphere, and, worst of all, costing me money! I decided he had to be eliminated.

About the fifth week, the host of the game called me to make sure I was coming. He did this as a regular courtesy to all the players. I told him I would not be attending his game anymore. Alarm registered in his voice as he asked why. I said I had enjoyed the game, but that one of the players was cheating and I didn't want to play in a dishonest game. Instantly he demanded to know who. I stalled, explaining to him that I was a newcomer and didn't want to make any waves. He pressed me further, encouraging me to speak out, and promising discreet, definitive action. Finally I told him that Charley was the culprit, and outlined the method by which he was shorting pots. He insisted that I return as scheduled and assured me he would watch Charley. If he confirmed my findings, he promised that Charley's playing days would be over. I readily accepted these conditions, making sure our host witnessed Charley in the act. Next week Charley was gone.

A few weeks later the host called me aside and asked me, in confidence, if anyone else was cheating. I assured him that with Charley gone the game was now clean. I saw no reason to have him get excited over the $100 that was still being regularly pinched—*that* player was too valuable and had to be protected.

Shiners

One of the oldest tricks in poker is the use of shiners (mirrors) to see an opponent's hand. Today, no one would be foolish enough to sit with a mirror behind him or, for that matter, anywhere in the room. Recently I witnessed an ingenious modification of the old shiner hanky-panky. A big loser in one of the California poker clubs decided to change his luck. He bought a stack of chips from the club and glued them together with epoxy resin. On the top chip he set in a tiny mirror. When he played, he always bought in for plenty of chips, and it was easy for him to conceal the stack with the shiner in the center of his piles of chips. He covered the shiner with chips matching the glued stack. When the deal came around to him, he wantonly adjusted a few chips, uncovering the tiny mirror submerged in the mass of chips. He could see every card he dealt! Needless to say, he became an uncommonly good player when he was the dealer.

Electronic Devices

When the reward warrants it, elaborate schemes can be engineered to fleece an unsuspecting pigeon. Some years back a group of hustlers found a mark worthy of such painstaking preparation. The retired president of a large company decided to vacation out west. One night he landed in a high-stakes public poker game. He played day and night, and before the week was out he had lost $50,000. Feeling angry and vengeful, he wired for money, canceled all pending appointments, and settled in. Though not a bad poker player, he was outclassed in this field. The locals checked him out and found that he was worth tens of millions—they nicknamed him J.P. In a futile attempt to get even, J.P. kept raising the stakes. The pros were willing to let him play as high as he wanted, but took a few additional precautions. Taking in the cardroom manager as a partner, they had J.P. watched from above through the "eye in the sky." From this angle his cards were plainly visible. They rigged up a wireless sound-transmitting system, the man above talking through a transmitter, the receiver a tiny battery-powered electrode that fit snugly into the ear canal. The ring of pros was constantly fed J.P.'s hole cards through the miniature receiver. J.P.

stayed the better part of a year, playing daily. He lost over $2,000,000! Finally he decided to admit defeat and move on. The pros involved in this caper have been living high off the hog ever since.

DICE

Loaded Dice

Bud is a corpulent man. His fleshy face sports a nose riddled with a road map of tortuous veins, signs of a good life and ample grog. Always dressed in a vested suit stretched tautly over his paunch and constantly peering over a pair of spectacles, he bears a remarkable resemblance to Benjamin Franklin. But Bud is far from being one of our Founding Fathers. He is a dice cheat— and a good one.

Standing with his enormous belly tucked snugly against the rail of the craps table, his stubby, milk-white fingers grope for a moment at his belt. The croupier passes him the dice. The nondescript woman on Bud's right has just sevened out. Bud selects two dice from those offered, shakes them furiously, and lets them fly. Moments later he sevens out and the dice pass on to the next player. The croupier collects Bud's $100 bet and adds it to the house stacks. With a gesture of resignation, Bud's heavy arms drop to his sides. Miss Plain on his right sympathetically gives his hand a squeeze. Effortlessly his practiced hand slips a die into hers. Moments later she departs. "Now let it work, evil thou art afoot" floats through Bud's consciousness, re-membering a line that he had memorized long ago from Shakespeare's *Julius Caesar*. Bud has successfully intro-duced a loaded die. Slipping it unseen from his belt, he had cast it into play while palming a house die in a well-padded crease of his hand. His female accomplice had now fled with the evidence. The dice had been passed and the next shooter was "comin' out" with the loaded die. Bud recalled supervising the engineering of the die —in every way identical in appearance to the house die. In every way except one—the die had been weighted on the face showing the 1. This causes the die to land with the weighted side down. If the 1 face is down, the 6 face is up. Bud knew that the die he had subsituted had been expertly constructed and would come up 6 with unexpected frequency.

"Place your bets," chanted the croupier. "They're comin' out." "A hundred on the eleven," Bud droned in his bass rumble. "You're on," the stick man said. "Eight, eight, the point is eight," he said as he scooped up Bud's C-note. "Buy the nine and ten for two hundred each," said Bud. "Ten, ten and he made it easy with a six-four. Four hundred to the gentleman with the vest." "Up two hundred," urged Bud. "Here they come—ten again, ten right back on that six and four. Pay the man eight hundred more. Shooter looking for an eight. Here they come. Two sixes, craps twelve, double field. Here they come again. Nine, nine, field roll nine. The gentleman's hot—three hundred more." "Press it up," ordered Bud. Within thirty minutes Bud waddled out with $22,000! In a routine dice check at the end of the shift the croupiers discovered the bogus die. Where it came from, and how, was a mystery. Anyone could have done it. The box man and pit bosses caught hell for lack of diligence and the dealers were grilled as the owners tried to unearth any conspiracies. Bud never returned. He travels all over the world with this little trick. Playing sparingly and only for brief periods, he has made a bundle.

To load dice, ordinary casino "cubes" are obtained through a contact working for the casino. Then one side is carefully weighted. Usually only one loaded die is brought into play. When this die is in action, the hustler will place the numbers likely to show. If the die is weighted to come up 6, each of the following have an equal chance of showing: 6–1, 6–2, 6–3, 6–4, 6–5, 6–6. Bud bought the 9 and 10 and bet 11 on the comeout roll. He would also make field bets.* To avoid suspicion he would bet on the pass line with the other players. He cleaned up!

Loaded dice have been around for ages. Rumor has it that fifteen years ago a local butcher would come into a downtown casino in Las Vegas during his lunch break. He would still have his apron on, appropriately garnished with various reddish hues. He was a big loser and everyone loved him. Then suddenly he went on a win streak. He played all over town, winning big everywhere. When he played, he always donned his apron. He said it brought him good luck. One day the secret of his good fortune was discovered. He was caught red-handed with no fewer than four sets of loaded dice tucked away in hidden pockets niftily concealed among the bloody stains of his apron. His playing days were over. A short time later he mysteriously disappeared. No one has heard from him since.

*　　*　　*

* A field bet pays even money if 3, 4, 9, 10, or 11 show. The field bettor doubles his money if the dice come up 2 or 12. With one die loaded to come up 6, four of the six likely combinations —9, 10, 11, and 12—are in the field and 12 pays double! You can see why Bud made field bets!

Money Scams

A number of clever swindles have been used at the craps table. The use of a "cap" is one of the better pranks. A cap is an empty shell that looks like a stack of four $25 chips, only it's hollow. The player and the craps dealer are in together as partners. The player bets what looks like $150. Really he is wagering only two $25 chips and the cap. If he wins the bet, his dealer-partner pays him $150. If he loses, the dealer collects the cap and chips and fills the empty cap with $100 chips. Now, when the player wins, he is given two $25 chips and the cap stuffed with $400. Adroitly the player removes the $100 chips, slips them in his pocket, and again bets the empty cap. The two men keep moving the cap in and out until they get their load.

The man responsible for controlling cheating at the craps table is the box man. That's that well-dressed, official-looking guy who camps at the middle of the table, guarding the stacks of chips. One play is to box out the box man. The dealer leans across the table to make change for $5. While the box man's view is momentarily obstructed, the dealer hands a stack of chips to his player-partner. Moments later, when the dealer straightens back up, all is normal—except for the two or three hundred that have vanished. This same technique is used to make change improperly or to allow a player, undetected, to add to his winning bet.

Chicanery is evident even for small amounts of money. An elderly pensioner had just the ticket. He would rush up to a crap game just as the dice were leaving the shooter's hand and yell, "Ten in the field," waving a $10 bill. A $1 bill was also in his hand on top of the ten, not visible to the box man. The box man would acknowledge the bet. If a field number came up, the player would take his $10 and leave. If the roll was not a field number, he would give the dealer the $1 bill. When challenged, he would say he only wanted to bet $1, having it out and ready. "But you said ten in the field," the box man would argue. "Well, ten *is* in the field. I was just rooting for a ten to win my dollar." After a while the box man would abandon the argument and have the old-timer booted out. But the old-timer had a few hundred before word spread.

An Unusual Coup

About a year ago I was idly watching a craps game. The dice were running against the players and everyone was losing. Then a new player arrived. He was a tan, healthy-looking man in his mid-sixties, with pearl-white closely cropped hair. He bet against the dice, playing the don't pass. He also placed the 4 and 5 and always bet on any craps (this bet wins on 2, 3, and 12). When he shot, he always held the dice the same way, one on top of the other with both aces (1's) up. Then he would weigh them in his hand a moment and cast off. The dice would fly out of his hands with tremendous velocity. One would ricochet all over the table. The other seemed to skid and spin around. He won consistently. The table had thinned out and he was now playing alone, betting hundreds and pressing his bets higher and higher. A crowd began to gather at the table but, unlike the usual crowd of spectators, this was a crowd of craps pit bosses. They sensed something was amiss. The dice seemed to be coming up on 1 an amazingly high percentage of the time. The player won every time 1–1, 1–2, 1–3, or 1–4 came up, and with heavy odds. 1–5 was no result. On balance, the player lost when 1–6 came up (7 out). When the man crossed the $15,000 mark, the pit boss changed all the dice. They were all checked out to see if they were loaded. They weren't. Still the man won. The way he was betting, the odds against him were quite high, yet he continued to win. At $50,000 the house finally pulled him up: "We don't know what you're doin', Mister, but we don't want your action anymore." The player cashed in his chips and quietly left. A few months later I heard the true story on this player. His win was no fluke. It turned out he had spent countless hours practicing throwing the dice. He had bought a craps table and spent an estimated ten years practicing. Then he was ready to tackle Vegas. When he threw the dice, he placed both 1's up. They would fly across the table. The bottom die would speed along only about an inch above the table. The top die would travel much higher, hitting the opposite rail and ricocheting wildly. The bottom die, however, would land in the crease between the table top and the far wall and then slide and spin. It would come up on 1 over eighty percent of the time! Phenomenal as it may seem, he had learned to cast the dice so that the die face *rarely turned,* spinning furiously but stopping consistently with the ace up. Miraculous . . . and legal! My informants tell me he has won over $1,000,000! Practice makes perfect!

Casino Cheating

Cheating by the house is exceedingly rare. Years ago you might have run into a pair of loaded dice at some of the smaller out-of-the-way casinos, but today, under the close scrutiny of the Nevada Gaming Commission, this is highly unlikely. Occasionally a casino will make an incorrect payoff, especially if the computation is complicated, but this is usually inadvertent. Sometimes a dealer may take matters into his own hands. An obnoxious drunk was playing at a large downtown Las Vegas casino. He was winning and swearing a blue streak. He bet large irregular stacks of differently colored chips, including $100, $25, $5, and $1 ones. The dealer was known to be exceptionally quick and accurate with figures. When the player won, the dealer would quickly slap together a pile of black, green, yellow, and white chips and give them to the player. Finally the box man, the man responsible for payoffs, turned to the dealer and asked what was going on. He could not keep up with the transactions. The dealer turned to him and said out of the corner of his mouth, "What's the difference? You know *he* isn't getting the best of it." The drunk was so repulsive, the box man let it go.

ROULETTE

Irregular Wheels

You may have heard stories about people recording the outcomes of countless thousands of spins of a roulette wheel and discovering a minute flaw in the wheel that affects the outcome, then taking advantage of it. This has been overdramatized. Most of the people who hang around every day, hovering over the European roulette wheels, are retired, daily wiling away the hours playing roulette with one system or another. I know of only two instances in which a wheel irregularity was successfully exploited. Both were in Europe, and only one was for big money. Extensive record-keeping is a total waste of time with the newer roulette wheels. They are perfectly balanced.

Past Posting

The most popular form of roulette cheating is past posting. The player makes his bet *after* the ball has fallen into a slot. Past posting is done in a variety of ways. Sometimes players continue to make bets after the croupier says, "No more bets." Sometimes a chip or two is added while the dealer is making another payoff. I have seen a player ask for change while the ball was spinning, and, as the dealer was getting change, the ball fell. Quickly the player placed a bet on the winning number before the distracted dealer could observe the outcome. The player successfully repeated this ruse three times in an hour, leaving with a tidy profit.

Partnerships

As in blackjack and craps, dealer-player partnerships can be set up in roulette. Again, past posting is the most common arrangement. The dealer allows his partner to make late bets. Incorrect payouts—plus a number of other tricks previously mentioned—are also applicable here.

SLOT MACHINES

False Coins

When I was a kid, I can remember occasionally putting slugs in pay-telephone and gumball machines. I recall with sheer delight the exhilaration when one worked, the gumball and prize magically falling into my hand. Perhaps similar boyhood experiences have inspired people to use false coins and slugs in slot machines. Whatever the cause, bogus coins and slugs are commonly encountered by slot caretakers when they empty the machines.

Not long ago I visited a casino in France just across the border from Geneva, Switzerland. A group of young Italians were playing the slots. Something about them struck me as suspicious. When they saw me staring in their direction, they moved to other machines, out of my view. Finally, overcome by curiosity, I went to my car and returned with a pair of high-power binoculars. Easing into an out-of-the-way corner of the casino, I zeroed in on them. They were playing at a 1-franc machine (about 25¢), but they were not putting francs in the slot. The coins they used were Italian 100-lire pieces worth about 8¢ each. Later I discovered that this Italian coin and the 1-franc piece were the same size. This is apparently a recurrent problem for French casinos. One French executive told me that on some nights half the money dropped into a machine is near-worthless lire.

One ex-slot mechanic I spoke with told me an even better story. In his youth, before he worked out more sophisticated methods for robbing slots, he used to tie a string of very strong flexible wire to a quarter and tackle the quarter slots. He would put in the quarter-on-a-string, pull the lever of the machine, then jerk the quarter from the jaws of the machine, playing for free. No slugs, no false coins, just free play. "Of course," he confessed, "I was just stringing them along in those days."

* * *

The Rhythm System

Slot machines are mechanically adjusted to pay out a percentage of the money taken in. A timing mechanism inside the machine controls the payout. Wizards of the slot machine can pull the machine's handle in a way that keeps tripping the timer and keeps the machine paying! They set up a certain rhythm to keep the timer falling into the same place. It doesn't take long for an expert to empty a slot machine completely.

The Pull-Through

A bit more strong-armed than the rhythm system is the pull-through. The hustler starts to pull the handle of the machine, then—at just the right time—he pulls the handle down hard, breaking the gear mechanism of the machine. The machine, now totally out of control, regularly keeps paying off.

Drilling Machines

The scam artist approaches his victim, takes a small drill from his pocket, and seconds later pierces the metal hide with a tiny hole. Slipping a fine wire through the hole, his knowing fingers guide it into the payout mechanism, freezing it in the payout position. In short order he empties the machine and hits the road.

Making Keys

Some rip-off artists prefer not to spend the time required to gradually empty a slot machine of its contents. They go for the big payoff—the jackpot. Setting a machine for a jackpot is a bit more difficult than just an ordinary payout. First, the thief forces semisolid wax into the lock of his target machine. When the wax sets, he withdraws a perfect mold. From this mold he makes a key that will open the slot. It takes three seconds for him to open the machine, set it for a jackpot, close and lock the machine, and disappear. His staid-looking female partner casually moves over from a nearby machine at which she has been playing for over an hour, and bingo! she takes off the jackpot.

Several months ago an incredible controversy erupted at a large Strip casino. A schoolteacher from Ohio dropped three Eisenhower dollars in a dollar machine. Wham! She hit a $75,000 jackpot. Whoopee! Only one small catch. Management had set the machine *not* to pay off a jackpot. A slot pro had made a key and changed the setting. But before his partner could get to the machine, Miss Schoolteacher had marched up, put in her $3, and won the jackpot. At first management refused to pay her the money. They said they had to "check things out." Our schoolteacher friend was as pure as Betty Crocker and in the end the casino was reluctantly forced to pay. Fitting.

Playing for Free

Besides setting a machine to deliver a jackpot, a machine can be set to work without a coin. Some cheats opt for this. The unknowing player puts in his coin and plays as usual, but the pro and his team just keep going through the motions, pulling the handle until the machine runs out of money. One machine at a large club in Reno was set like this for over a year. The hustler's squad came in daily and took off the machine. Their tampering was finally discovered when a tourist put in a quarter and got three oranges, but nary a farthing dropped into the pay slot. When she protested, the casino opened the machine and found it empty!

Old Machines vs. New

It is much more difficult for slot pros to tamper with the new electronic slot machines. Rhythm and pull-through methods don't work and they are more difficult to set. For the moment the cheats have gone back to the drawing board, or are tackling the European and African casinos, where old-style machines are still being used.

KENO

Cheating at keno is unknown today. But not long ago, in the days prior to electronic time-stamping and sophisticated casino-surveillance techniques, some big scores were made. A clerk would make out a ticket while the numbers were being called, affix a phony time stamp, and his partner would calmly come up and collect $25,000.

As long as there is gambling, there will be cheating. Old cheats are constantly being culled from the casino floors and new ones are being turned out. Cheating is a felony punishable by fine and/or imprisonment. There are easier and safer ways to make a living.

15

On Gambling and Gamblers

Luck

The ruddy-faced man with silver-gray hair, named Ben, sat bleary-eyed at the blackjack table. Small red veins spread across the bridge of his nose like tiny red rivers, a sign of long-standing, excessive alcoholic intake. Normally a $5 bettor, today he felt lucky and bought in for $300. Immediately he began to fortify his courage with double Scotches. His playing tactic was never to break. Ben would stand on 12 or higher, regardless of the dealer's up card. He would not double down and never split pairs, except for aces. Playing this way, the player disadvantage exceeds eight percent, but today Ben was winning. As his chips piled up, his drinking pace increased, dousing his fears. He parlayed his bets up to the house limit—$2,000 per hand. Still he won. When I stumbled across the scene of Ben's game, he had been in action just over an hour and was $16,000 winners. I watched for half an hour, while he consumed six doubles, and doubled his mound of chips. Ben was well on his way to dual record—12 doubles and $32,000 per hour—both definitely world-record paces. His luck was uncanny.

After dinner, I returned to his game. An enormous crowd had gathered. His $100 chips had been replaced with $500 chips. I quickly counted his stacks. It was unbelievable. He now had $78,000 and was still gulping down doubles with the rapidity of a chain smoker. A flashy woman had joined him, and he was liberally showering her with $100 chips, which she stuffed away. At this point Ben could hardly see, and his new-found filly would help him read his hands. Still he won. There's no telling how much he'd had to drink. I had personally witnessed eight doubles and had missed three hours of play. He now had $88,000 piled in huge, irregular stacks of $500 chips.

Suddenly he collapsed into his chips, spraying them everywhere. The alert pit bosses and security guards collected them. Ben was out cold. Helplessly, the pit crew was fanning him with towels, hoping to revive him, but to no avail. An iced cloth on his face also had no effect. Finally the crew gave up. Ben was obviously "down for the count" and would not waken for hours. The house doctor confirmed the drunken stupor. They carted Ben off to his room, locking up the $88,000 in the cashier's cage. He slept for 18 hours. When he awoke, his room was adorned with fresh flowers, champagne, and other little trinkets at the request of the casino. Puzzled, he struggled down to the casino, his head throbbing with a whopping hangover. He was warmly greeted and informed that his money had been safely deposited in the casino vault. "What money?" he asked. The executives laughed nervously. "Why, the eighty-eight thousand you won last night." "I won what?" Ben shrieked. "My God!" The man had no recollection of the previous evening. All he could remember was feeling lucky, buying in for $300, and winning a few hands. The rest was a blank. He filled his suitcase with the loot, put $500 in an envelope for the dealers, and left like a startled hare. To my knowledge, he has never returned to Las Vegas, having found his pot of gold at the end of a well-liquored rainbow.

Events like this strike a resonant chord in the depths of a gambler's soul. It's the big chance, the lucky streak, that drives the sporadic gambler. But for some, gambling assumes deeper psychological significance. Sure, they still get off on the excitement, but for the degenerate gambler, losing fills a need. Having low self-esteem, he unconsciously desires to punish himself. He does this by losing. Only when he's lost everything he has is he pacified. Then he can begin to feel good about himself. After all, he has withstood all this grief and come out the other side, so for a fleeting moment he is appeased. The reprieve is short; he needs constant doses. This masochistic behavior is a self-defeating sickness often leading to financial and psychic ruin, and those caught on this treadmill are often refractory even to intensive psychotherapeutic efforts.

Why Most Professional Gamblers Have No Money

A variant of this malady can be found amid professional circles. I know many people who play poker for a living. As soon as they accumulate a little money they are off to the race track, bucking seventeen percent odds! Others blow their dough on sports betting, where they have five percent the worst of it. How can someone who survives by making the most of a small edge go up against such propositions, knowing he must ultimately lose? Some feel guilty about their livelihood. Deep down they think they should be making a "respectable" living and feel bad about the "dirty" money. As a professional gambler friend of mine succinctly put it, "They have to fuck off those ill-begotten gains. Then they feel clean again." This type of behavior is surprisingly common. Most pros are constantly in and out of money. They make a few bucks and then promptly lose it, living hand to mouth most of their lives. A few overcome the moral issues and look at gambling as a job. They only get involved when they have the best of it. Action doesn't interest them as much as income. They pick their spots and put in their hours. Disciplined and well managed, they are always favorites, both feared and envied by other players. It's an ego trip to beat these experts, and many players throw away their money trying. Poker, Ping-Pong, chess, checkers, dominoes, backgammon, or tic-tac-toe—if they will play it with you, you don't stand a chance. These refined game players are an amazing breed. They know their limitations, but will bet on anything when they think they hold the whip hand. I have seen one of these prodigies play Ping-Pong for $500 a game! There was no way his opponent could win.

They Bet on Anything

In Las Vegas, people bet on anything. One day I was having lunch with a group of big bookmakers. We were at a delicatessen and I was hungry and packing the food away. One of the group studied me inquisitively as I ate. "You always eat like this?" he teased. I told him, as I polished off a second order of blintzes, that I usually had a pretty good appetite. His eyes opened wider as I tackled a bagel with cream cheese and a third glass of freshly squeezed orange juice. When I ordered a plate of cold cuts and some chopped liver, he could contain himself no longer. "I think we've got a challenger on our hands," he said. "Of course, I'd like to see a few breakfasts and maybe a dinner or two to make a more accurate line, but right now I'd have to make him a three-blintz favorite over Big Sid." "Three blintzes over Sid!" exclaimed another member of the group. "That's way too high. Sure, the man can eat, but Sid is no slouch." "You might be right," the other man countered. "All right, two and a half blintzes, six to five pick 'em." I found the entire conversation very amusing and was laughing in my orange juice. I ate with this group on a number of other occasions. There were usually a few strange faces at the tables and I met many colorful characters. I always seemed to be in rare form, eating-wise, and out-ate everyone at the table.

But one day a rotund affable man joined us and really started putting it away. For openers, he had six eggs and a rye bread, washed down by a quart of orange juice. This was no patsy. Instinctively, I knew I was up against the fabled Big Sid. I started off with a three-egg omelet, some sliced beefsteak tomatoes, an order of whitefish, two bagels with cream cheese, and matched his quart of orange juice. Slowing down only slightly, Sid chomped on a few pickles and devoured a double order of marinated herring. I countered with an order of blintzes and a glass of milk. The contest was a toss-up, when Sid suddenly rose. After a horrendous belch, he whimpered that his ulcer was acting up again and he was going to have to cut his lunch short. I looked up from the plate of leftovers I was finishing off in time to see Sid waddle away. One of the group laughed derisively and said, "What a letdown! My horse pulled up lame in the stretch," and solemnly handed $300 to the gentleman on his right. Unbeknownst to either Sid or myself, these guys had staged an eating contest with $300 riding on the outcome. Next day, when Sid heard what had happened, he was furious. "How come no one told me?" he cried. "If I'd a known there was money on me, I could've eaten another dozen eggs." I knew I couldn't have and was glad I had had no knowledge of the bet.

Even in the casinos, amazing things happen when it comes to covering bets. An eighty-five-year-old man was playing craps. Withered, his height stunted with age, he could hardly see over the edge of the table. But he was a spry old codger and he threw the dice with gusto, banging up against the side of the table with each roll. He was very vocal, shrieking with glee when he won and cursing if he lost. Well, he had a pretty good run going and was getting really excited. Making yet another point, he let out a holler, but to everyone's astonishment the old salt's false teeth came flying out of his mouth, landing solidly on the pass line. A pit boss in his early sixties had been watching the action and reacted with lightning-quick reflexes. In a flash he whipped out his own dentures, placed them next to the player's set, and said, "You're faded!"

Although you can get a bet down on almost anything in this gambling oasis, smart gamblers don't gamble. They'll bet with you on anything when they know they have the best of it, but they won't even go for a 50–50 proposition. If you are to be a winner, you must stifle the impulse to gamble. Let people call you a tightwad or anything else they care to, you'll have the money when it's all over. One casino executive put it to me this way: "You have about as much gamble in you as a snail." "Coming from you," I said, "that's the nicest compliment I've had since I started coming here."

16

*Managing Stress
while Gambling*

Gambling is full of stress, and gamblers notoriously have difficulties in dealing with tension. The winning gambler must learn to manage the inevitable stress and strain of playing. Winning demands awareness, alertness, decisiveness, and clear thought. Body and mind must be integrated. Diet, sleep, exercise, and relaxation techniques are fundamental to consistent winning.

Diet

What and when you eat influence how you feel. In addition to affecting long-term health, diet can have profound short-term affects on mental attitude. The primary cause of transient mood swings is changes in blood sugar. If you have ever had the misfortune of having a diabetes test (as I have) you know how fluctuations in blood sugar affect you. First you fast for twelve hours. This leaves you hungry, light-headed, slightly weak, and irritable. Then you drink 100 grams of the most godawful, sickeningly sweet stuff you have ever tasted, euphemistically called Glucola. When the nausea subsides, you have about a fifteen-minute reprieve before the concoction hits you. As your blood sugar skyrockets, you get a rush of nervous energy. Your body reacts to this jolt of sugar by putting out large quantities of insulin. Blood sugar plummets as the insulin drives the sugar into storage. This rapid drop makes you irascible, twitchy, and shaky. Your nerves are shattered at the slightest provocation. Attention span shortens and concentration fails. Weak, sweaty, and depressed, you welcome the end of the test.

The same thing can happen when you are playing. Eager, you may play before breakfast. Starving, you go for some of those good pancakes with lots of butter and syrup and maybe a few strips of bacon. Bloated, you return to the tables. After a while your concentration begins to fail. The jitters set in. You feel irritable and angry. The casino seems noisy, the cocktail waitresses disturbing, and the pit bosses grouchy. You've set yourself up to be bagged. You can't think, your hands are shaking, and your stomach is churning while the sugar and insulin battle it out. When you lose, it should be no surprise. Your system cannot take this chemical insult and perform up to expectation. A high-protein, low-carbohydrate diet is preferable. Protein is slowly broken down and gradually assimilated into your body. The blood sugar rises and falls slowly from proteins, giving you an increased usable energy source over a long period. This provides the fuel you need for proper play without taxing your nerves.

Frequent small meals make me feel better than large feasts. I eat four or five small servings daily when playing. This way my stomach doesn't feel bloated and I don't have that heavy, lethargic feeling that comes from overeating. Milk is an excellent protein supplement between meals.

Alcohol is anathema to play. It dulls senses, clouds concentration, and destroys self-discipline. In addition, medical studies show that alcohol stimulates aggressive behavior. The tendency is to become combative with the dealers and house men. We have seen how such behavior is self-defeating. Booze and cards just don't mix, so use milk for oral gratification.

Sleep

It is often difficult to sleep in tension-packed situations. Some players lose sleep when they have lost, others lose sleep after a win. Although a physiological need for sleep has not been established, I certainly feel a lot better after having a little. Most players agree— they tend to lose when tired.

Sleep can be fickle. It can elude you even when you've been up for countless hours and your body is screaming for it. The trick is to be able to shut off your mind. The damn thing just keeps reviewing every hand, every decision, every interaction in an endless progression.

An understanding of your biological clock, that inner timepiece which regulates your body processes, will help you control your sleeping pattern. Undoubtedly you are aware of varying amounts of energy at different times of the day. Some of us function best in the morning, others late at night. A "lark" is a person who awakens refreshed and full of vitality. As the day progresses, his energy slowly wanes like a clock running down. By evening, he has shot his wad and collapses around 10:00 P.M. The "owl" type person is a slow starter. By noon he is still having trouble focusing. But by mid-afternoon he starts to perk up. His energy level continues to climb through the evening and by midnight he's in fourth gear. He peaks out about 2:00 A.M. and falls asleep about an hour later. If you are a lark, best results will be obtained by playing early in the day; owls do best in the evening and around the witching hour. Pattern your playing time to your body rhythm.

Each time you feel sleepy, record the time. After a week or so a pattern will emerge. I get sleepy each night at 7:30 P.M., 9:00 P.M., 10:30 P.M. and midnight. The trick is to catch your sleepy wave when trying to sleep. If you know you are going to get sleepy at a given time, get in bed about fifteen minutes before hand and distract yourself by reading or watching television. Do this for ten minutes. Then turn out the lights, lie on your back, and breathe deeply and slowly through your nose. Let the breath flow into your abdomen, exhale fully, then wait until the next breath comes. Don't worry—it always comes, but the waiting is important. Concentrate on your breathing. As you do this, your sleepy wave will overtake you. By focusing on your breathing and relaxing in coordination with a bottoming out of your energy level, you will sleep. This technique can be applied any time you want to sleep. Morning or afternoon naps can be scheduled with this knowledge of your internal rhythm. Many players find short naps (30–45 minutes) beneficial prior to playing. Let your body tell you what it needs, then listen to it. If you try to press too hard, it may rebel, so pamper yourself.

Another useful technique to induce sleep is a step-by-step relaxation process. While lying on your back, concentrate on your feet. Imagine they are warm and heavy. Concentrate on relaxing them. Repeat to yourself, "My feet are warm and heavy; my feet are very pleasantly and deeply relaxed." Once your feet are fully relaxed, visualize a wave of relaxation moving slowly up your body, starting from your feet. Slowly, let it spread into your calves, then up into your knees and thighs, spreading gradually like ripples in a warm pool. Let this wave progress up your entire body, melting away tension as it goes, leaving your body limp in its wake. Take extra time on your neck and shoulders. Most people hold their tension in this region.

The entire exercise should take about twenty minutes. When completed, you may choose from two alternatives. First, you can opt for sleep. With muscle tension greatly reduced, say to yourself, "My body and mind are very relaxed; my breath is calm and even— it sleeps me." Coordinate this with the sleepy part of your cycle, and you will be gone. A second course is to awake and play. To do this, think: "My mind and body are clear; I feel refreshed and alert. Energy is flowing through my body." Slowly open your eyes after a minute or two for optimum results. Try to time your waking with the high-energy part of your cycle.

Master these techniques and you will be able to turn your mind on or off at will. There will be times when you'll find this ability invaluable, not only in gambling, but also during other stressful periods of your life.

Exercise

Sitting hunched over a blackjack table or spending hours in a chair playing poker leads to stiff muscles. Sometimes it feels as though I need to be unfolded in order to straighten up after a long poker session. Daily exercise helps get out the kinks and clears the mind. Most helpful are stretching activities—yoga, swimming, or jogging. I find yoga and swimming most practical. Jogging in 120° heat is just not my cup of tea. The resort hotels feature beautiful big swimming pools, and I spend about a half an hour a day limbering up in the refreshing coolness of their waters. Yoga is easily practiced in the hotel room. For me, the best time is right after awakening, to start my energy flowing. Both swimming and yoga relax my mind as well as my body, and tend to clear my head, leaving me invigorated and alert, once again ready for the wars.

Relaxation

Stretching exercises help relieve muscle tension but should be complemented by regular periods of deep muscle relaxation. This is best accomplished by combining physical aids with relaxation techniques.

The big hotels house lavish health clubs, complete with saunas, steam rooms, whirlpools, and cold baths. Masseurs and masseuses are readily available. The sauna, whirlpool, cold bath, and massage combination is dynamite! It's hard to stay uptight after this barrage. But still, the level of relaxation is incomplete.

Two exercises are useful to complete the job. The first, known as Jacobson Relaxation Training, was developed in the 1930s and has been successfully used by notables such as Senator William Proxmire to master profound muscle relaxation. This technique emphasizes the contrast between tension and relaxation. To do it, isometrically tense a muscle group (see Table 11) for three to five seconds, focusing all your attention on how this tension *feels*. Then relax completely. Concentrate on how these muscles feel when relaxed, noting the difference between tension and relaxation. The relaxation phase should last about thirty to forty seconds. Repeat this tension-relaxation cycle twice for each muscle group. It takes about thirty minutes to get around your whole body. Then spend five minutes feeling your body in total relaxation. Focus on how it feels to be completely relaxed. Slowly open your eyes, spend another minute or so feeling renewed energy course through your body, and gradually get up.

TABLE 11 *

Muscle Groups in Desired Order	How to Tense
1. Right hand and forearm	1. Make a tight fist.
2. Right biceps	2. Push your elbow against the bed with arm bent at 90° angle.
3. Left hand and forearm	3. Same as (1)
4. Left biceps	4. Same as (2)
5. Forehead	5. Lift your eyebrows as high as you can.
6. Face	6. Squint your eyes very tightly and wrinkle up your nose.
7. Jaw	7. Bite down hard with your teeth and pull back the corners of your mouth.
8. Neck	8. Pull your chin down toward your chest but prevent it from

* Adapted from *Progressive Relaxation Training: A Manual for the Helping Professions* by Douglas A. Bernstein and Thomas E. Borkovec; copyright © 1973 by Research Press, Champaign, Illinois.

Muscle Groups in Desired Order	How to Tense
	actually touching. Come as close to your chest as possible without touching.
9. Shoulders and chest	9. Pull your shoulder blades together after first inhaling deeply.
10. Abdomen	10. Make your stomach hard.
11. Right upper leg	11. Make your thigh hard.
12. Right lower leg	12. Bring your toes up toward your head.
13. Right foot	13. Curl your toes downward.
14. Left upper leg	14. Same as (11)
15. Left lower leg	15. Same as (12)
16. Left foot	16. Same as (13)

The second exercise is a takeoff on the breathing technique described in the section on sleep. Lie on your back, breathing deeply through your nose into your abdomen, and wait after each exhalation until the next breath comes. Now concentrate as you breathe to those parts of your body that feel especially tense. For me it's my neck and shoulders. Imagine your breath flowing through your nostrils and going directly into a sore spot. When you exhale, visualize your breath coming right out of the area of tension, like a jet of air. Each inhalation fills the tense area like a warm flowing stream, and each exhalation empties it of tension. You can feel the sore spots inflate and deflate with each breath. When one place relaxes, move on to the next. Continue until you have gotten them all. Spend about five minutes in this state of total relaxation, then slowly mobilize yourself.

Another useful relaxation technique is meditation. Those familiar with transcendental meditation (T.M.)

know its salubrious effects. In T.M., the initiate is given a mantra, an Indian word that he repeats over and over, while sitting comfortably with eyes closed. At first outside thoughts will intrude, but the student is encouraged to keep going back to his mantra. This is quickly learned and the results are often dramatic. Pulse and respiration rate slow, blood pressure falls, and skin temperature rises—all signs of deep relaxation. Sessions last twenty minutes, leaving you relaxed, refreshed, and mentally alert. Failing a mantra, a similar result can be achieved by counting your breaths. Count each inhalation and exhalation. When you reach ten, start over again, at one. Still another method is to repeat over and over to yourself the number one. With each of these variations you will reach the same end point.

If tension overtakes me while I'm playing (usually when I'm losing), I'll take a moment out, close my eyes and clear my head without even leaving the table. I simply sit out a couple of decks and concentrate on relaxing. It works! I've made some incredible comebacks after checking out like this for a few minutes.

You can do a lot to help your body in its quest for serenity. Limit the length of your trips to a week. Longer trips tend to wear on you, and you will lose efficiency. Also, remember to limit your blackjack sessions to forty-five minutes. Longer sessions really take it out of you, so don't tax your system unduly.

It's important to realize you don't have to play. Far too many players put in too many hours. You can always find a game when *you* are ready and in top form, so only play when you feel right. Don't play if you're tired and don't play "for the hell of it." If you have that sinking feeling when you sit down and feel you are going to lose, quit at once! No reason to tempt fate. My experience is that when I think I'm going to lose, I do! Play to win, approaching the game in a cool, calm manner, your objective clearly at hand. No need to impress others or show off; direct all your attention toward that highly coveted reward—money! Pamper yourself like a top athlete, and make your session the main event.

Bring an adequate bankroll. You don't need the aggravation of playing on short money.

Withdraw after a loss until your confidence and mental well-balance return. Don't press. Continually remind yourself that you have all the time in the world.

Remember, you have the upper hand unless you blow it. Combine proper diet, exercise, and relaxation with confidence, discipline, and self-control, and Las Vegas is your oyster. So be careful not to lose the pearl once you pry it loose.

Afterword

And so time passes. Each trip I make I fear will be my last, but I continue to play, unmolested. How long can it last? I'm beginning to think, indefinitely. As long as the pit bosses are motivated, for one or another reason, to maintain contact with me rather than sever relations, I remain safe. After hundreds of hours of big play, I have not been barred from one casino in the entire state of Nevada. I haven't yet played in over half of them. There are still many fertile fields to plow. Artfully directed and well disciplined, a polished newcomer has limitless potential.

About the Author

For the last decade, Ian Andersen has made his living gambling in Las Vegas. Few persons, if any, have consistently made as much money. An expert on all casino games, Mr. Andersen got his start while in college, by observing a professional poker player. By the time he was in graduate school, the author was nicely supplementing his otherwise meager income with his poker earnings. But poker isn't a casino game, and since the casinos had more money than his friends, he took up blackjack, in which the winning potential is limitless.

Before committing his life to gambling, however, Andersen thoroughly researched not only gambling games but other factors that have an acute bearing on the results achieved: control of mind and body, nutrition, exercise, and relaxation.

Considered by many to be the best active blackjack player in the world, Ian Andersen regularly continues to win at his chosen profession. And he still is an honored guest at every casino in Las Vegas.